D1015692

"A critical component of any winning business is an HR function that improves business results. I highly recommend this book to HR and business leaders everywhere."

—WILLIAM S. ALLEN, SENIOR VP, GROUP HR, AP MOLLER-MAERSK AS,
COPENHAGEN, DENMARK

"Got business? This book does. By asking (and answering) the tough questions about HR relevance for line managers, shareholders, and customers, readers will clearly understand the why, how, and what of HR transformation."

—RICH BAIRD, JOINT U.S. AND GLOBAL LEADER,
ADVISORY PEOPLE AND CHANGE, PwC

"Wow, they have done it! Many HR shops need transformation but don't have the answers. This book is the roadmap, answers the questions, provides the rationale, and describes how HR transformations should unfold. Read it, but better yet—do it!"

—RICHARD W. BEATTY, RUTGERS UNIVERSITY,
COAUTHOR OF *THE DIFFERENTIATED WORKFORCE*

"A must read for an HR team that wants to add the most value to the business."

—BOB BLOSS, HR EXECUTIVE VICE PRESIDENT, HALLMARK

"A thoughtful and practical guide that will help leaders navigate some of the most important decisions about building the HR organization of the future."

—JOHN BOUDREAU, USC MARSHALL,
COAUTHOR OF *INVESTING IN PEOPLE* AND *BEYOND HR*

"Two bangs for your hard-earned buck. First, a very strong summary of the key tenets of the most important HR thinking. Second, highly practical examples of what to do and—even more importantly—what NOT to do when embarking upon transformation."

—REG BULL, FORMER CHIEF HR OFFICER, LG ELECTRONICS, SEOUL,
SOUTH KOREA

"Dave Ulrich and his colleagues have, over the past two decades, fundamentally changed the way we view HR. This work will change the way we *think* about HR and what we *do* with it as we build lasting, competitive organizations in a complex environment."

—RALPH CHRISTENSEN, AUTHOR OF *ROADMAP TO STRATEGIC HR* AND
HEAD OF HR, LDS CHURCH

"This practical, thoughtful, well-researched book provides priceless insights on the most pressing issue: how to effectively leverage people to deliver value amidst turmoil. In an economy anxious to weed out the weak, no HR executive can afford to miss this book."

—Bill Conaty, retired Senior VP HR, GE, Conaty Consulting LLC

"*HR Transformation* is refreshing. Ulrich, et al., have given us a clear vision of where the HR function ought to go next. The big ideas are presented in a straightforward way to ensure HR is pointed in the right direction long after you've put down the book."

—David Creelman, CEO, Creelman Research

"The authors nail the seminal question in the first pages when they state that the biggest challenge for HR professionals is to 'help their respective organizations succeed.' Frankly, most leaders don't care about HR, nor should they if HR doesn't add value."

—Jac Fitz-Enz, CEO of Human Capital Source,
author of *The ROI of Human Capital*

"Based on knowledge, experience, research, and wisdom, the authors have produced an incredibly practical volume. The four case studies add to the richness and usefulness."

—Fred K. Foulkes, Director, HR Policy Institute,
Boston University

"This is an indispensable handbook for the HR leader looking to help the business succeed, a chronicle of the silent revolution taking place in some of the world's leading HR functions, with systematic steps to transform the function and create real value."

—Diane J. Gherson, Vice President HR, Global Business Services
and Recruitment, IBM

"Powerful, practical answers to the critical why, what, and how questions that fuel any high-impact HR transformation! A must-have map for any executive in turbulent times."

—Hal Gregersen, Professor of Leadership, INSEAD, and
coauthor of *It Starts with One*

"A must-read for any HR leader looking to drive value and contribution to the business! This book is a practical guide for instituting complete organizational transformation, balancing theory, practice, and application in a no-nonsense, action-oriented way."

—Linda Hlavac, Senior VP, Human Resources, LexisNexis, US

"Good business books give you ideas; great books tell you what to do with them. *HR Transformation* integrates critical ideas with practical tools to answer the 'so what do I actually do?' question. Above all it starts where HR needs to start: with the business."

—NICK HOLLEY, DIRECTOR OF THE HR CENTRE OF EXCELLENCE, HENLEY BUSINESS SCHOOL

"If more candidates for the largest HR positions in the world 'had the horses' to live up to the promise of the function outlined in this book, my job would be a lot easier. Thankfully, there is an increasing number of great HR leaders who get this stuff."

—HAROLD E JOHNSON, KORN/FERRY INTERNATIONAL, MANAGING DIRECTOR, CLIENT DEVELOPMENT

"It's clear that five good thinkers spent a great deal of time debating the issues raised in this book, and then collaborated with colleagues to gather essential feedback. This is a great guide with excellent case studies that make the theory come to life."

—BEVERLY KAYE, CEO/FOUNDER, CSI, AND COAUTHOR OF *LOVE 'EM OR LOSE 'EM*

"There has never been a better time for HR professionals to help business leaders. A great, compelling read that delivers an integrated, aligned, and innovative approach to transforming HR and thereby transforming the business."

—STEPHEN KELLY, GROUP HR DIRECTOR, LOGICA

"In the past, these authors have changed the way people think about the roles, goals, and even the raison d'être of HR. Here, building on their previous work, they offer valuable, practical advice on transforming HR to bring maximum value to stakeholders."

—STEVE KERR, AUTHOR OF *REWARD SYSTEMS* AND FORMER CLO OF GOLDMAN SACHS AND GE

"This book is a must read for every HR professional. Its premise—that HR transformation is not about doing HR better, but rather building business success—is an appropriate challenge and wake-up call for our function."

—BOB LANDIS, SENIOR VP OF PERSONNEL AND ORGANIZATION, MARS CHOCOLATE

"*HR Transformation* has it right! It provides a great approach to use in transforming HR. Useful case studies as well as great 'how to do it' guidance."

—EDWARD E. LAWLER, AUTHOR OF *ACHIEVING EXCELLENCE IN HUMAN RESOURCES MANAGEMENT*

"In these turbulent times we live in, *HR Transformation* has arrived just in time. Human resources is being called upon to contribute to the business like never before and the RBL Group has provided a proven, practical roadmap to success."

—Keith Lawrence, Director Human Resources, P&G

"A distinctive guide for 21st-century HR leadership. *HR Transformation* shows how HR can help organizations succeed, combining a positive vision with practical tools, and truly raises the bar higher for all HR professionals."

—John Lynch, Senior VP, Human Resources, GE

"This book starts the journey to truly upgrade the HR profession. Against a backdrop of increased complexity, *HR Transformation* highlights the importance of HR connecting with business line managers, customers, and investors."

—Tony McCarthy, Chief of People and Organisational Effectiveness, British Airways

"In every profession, 20 percent of the people in that profession produce 80 percent of the great work. Reading this book will help move you into the 20 percent category for HR."

—Debbie McGrath, CEO, HR.com

"This book finally gives clarity to what 'HR transformation' really means. The core message: HR exists to grow the business! This is a primer for anyone serious about making HR relevant in today's business."

—Paul McKinnon, Head of HR, Citigroup

"What a great contribution to HR thinking and performance! Not only does *HR Transformation* provide a practical and insightful step-by-step guide to HR redesign, it challenges us to rethink who we are, what we do, and why we do it. Essential reading."

—Heather Miles, General Manager, Group People, Westpac Banking Corporation

"A very insightful and practical handbook. It is a must for CEOs and business and HR managers who want to transform HR to maximize the tangible business results from their HR investments. I will buy several copies for the Nokia HR team."

—Hallstein Moerk, Executive VP of HR, Nokia

"Dave Ulrich has been a pioneer in leading HR practitioners to think, act, and be increasingly progressive in how we add value. He and his colleagues are now providing us a blueprint to transform HR."

—Moheet Nagrath, Global Human Resources Officer, The Procter & Gamble Company

"Turbulent economic times call for an enhanced focus on HR results. A healthy paranoia that makes us strive for 'the little extra' in the attempt not to be left behind will be the key to excellence in the coming years."

—SANNE JUUL NIELSEN, MANAGING DIRECTOR,
DANISH TECHNOLOGICAL INSTITUTE, C&T

"Transformations have always happened through those who exemplify character, credibility, and capability. This book captures these very well and emphasizes that successful transformation is judged by business strategy, which shapes competitive capability."

—K. RAMKUMAR, EXECUTIVE DIRECTOR,
ICICI BANK, MUMBAI

"This is the guide leaders have been searching for—a clearly articulated model, candid cases, and tools ready for application. Critics have been calling for HR transformation for years. This is the first book that provides the what, how, and who to make it happen."

—NANCY A. REARDON, SENIOR VP AND CHIEF HR AND
COMMUNICATIONS OFFICER, CAMPBELL SOUP COMPANY

"This book is an invaluable roadmap for any HR leader or CEO looking to transform the contribution and effectiveness of HR. Clarify an organization's unique identity and capabilities to unlock the true opportunity for HR to drive improved business results."

—SUSIE ROBINSON, SENIOR VP HR, DHL SUPPLY CHAIN, UK IRELAND,
EEMEA, AND EUROPE

"This book identifies the challenges facing HR and provides practical ways to meet those challenges. To add value and succeed HR must be aligned around the business strategy. It sounds simple yet so many HR professionals find it hard to do."

—NEIL RODEN, GROUP DIRECTOR, HUMAN RESOURCES,
ROYAL BANK OF SCOTLAND

"A timely and relevant message to HR professionals, educators, and business leaders that should be taken seriously now. If it isn't, HR will be left in the back room."

—JUDY ROSENBLUM, A FOUNDER OF DUKE CORPORATE EDUCATION

"*HR Transformation* is a call to action for HR professionals and line managers everywhere. The practical advice and tools offered in this book will help leaders assess how well they are leveraging their organization's most important asset: people."

—MATT SCHUYLER, CHIEF HR OFFICER, CAPITAL ONE

"*HR Transformation* is not just a handbook but a manifesto for deliberately altering the DNA of the HR function, its mission, and, importantly, what it is charged with delivering. The book is a timely and very worthwhile read for any HR executive."

—Dennis W. Shuler, Executive VP and Chief HR Officer,
The Walt Disney Company

"Practical knowledge that human resources professionals can put to use immediately. Given the importance and relevance of strategic HR, the perspective here is spot-on, and the information provided is transferable and can be applied in a wide range of industries."

—Jill Smart, Head of HR, Accenture

"The authors brilliantly lay out the business case for transforming HR from an administrative department to strategic executioner. A great book for all executives."

—Mark R. Thomas, VP, HR and OD,
Greater Baltimore Medical Center

"Just when we believe we've arrived, these authors lead us to clearly see that there's yet another level to reach and an order to go with it. Going beyond theory, this book provides a practical and proven process for transforming HR."

—Dean Weatherford, Advisor, Abu Dhabi Investment Authority

"Dave Ulrich and his colleagues have conducted more research on HR competencies and have worked with more HR functions in guiding HR transformations than anyone else in the world. This is a must-read.

—Patrick M. Wright, W. J. Conaty GE Professor of Strategic HR,
ILR, Cornell University

"Insightful and practical! A must-read for HR and business leaders in emerging economies who strive to manage and develop talent for hyper business growth."

—Arthur Yeung, Associate Dean of China Europe International
Business School

Transformation

Building Human Resources
from the Outside In

DAVE ULRICH   JUSTIN ALLEN
WAYNE BROCKBANK   JON YOUNGER   MARK NYMAN

New York   Chicago   San Francisco   Lisbon   London   Madrid   Mexico City
Milan   New Delhi   San Juan   Seoul   Singapore   Sydney   Toronto

The McGraw·Hill Companies

Library of Congress Cataloging-in-Publication Data

HR transformation: building human resources from the outside in / Dave Ulrich ... [et al.]. —
  1st ed.
      p.   cm. — (RBL Institute HR leadership series)
    Includes index.
    ISBN 0-07-163870-9
    1. Personnel management.   2. Personnel departments.   I. Ulrich, David, 1953–

  HF5549.H6584   2009
  658.3'01—dc22   2009026614

Copyright © 2009 by The RBL Institute. All rights reserved. Printed in the United States of
America. Except as permitted under the United States Copyright Act of 1976, no part of this
publication may be reproduced or distributed in any form or by any means, or stored in a
database or retrieval system, without the prior written permission of the publisher.

      5 6 7 8 9 10 11 12 13 14 15 16 17 18 19 20 21 22 23 24   WFR/WFR 0

ISBN   978-0-07-163870-8
MHID   0-07-163870-9

McGraw-Hill books are available at special quantity discounts to use as premiums and sales
promotions, or for use in corporate training programs. To contact a representative please
e-mail us at bulksales@mcgraw-hill.com.

CONTENTS

ACKNOWLEDGMENTS

We are greatly indebted to many people who have made this work possible. While it is impossible to formally acknowledge everyone who has contributed to this book from its inception to its final realization, we wish to begin by thanking the human resources professionals in companies and conferences where we test and improve our ideas.

We owe special thanks to members of The RBL Institute for their ongoing support, collaboration, and ideas. We specifically highlight four Institute members in this work, but we owe a thorough thanks to each of our members, all of whom continue to add invaluable insights in our Think Tank Sessions and Mini-Forums where we test our ideas and learn from their questions and best practices. We have been fortunate to learn from thought leaders in leading firms who have taught us by their creation and application of ideas.

We also owe a special thanks to Hilary Powers who is our ever-gracious and insightful editor and "write" knight.

We are grateful to McGraw-Hill for allowing us to publish with them and particularly to Michele Wells who has been most helpful.

We are grateful for our HR colleagues who have informed our thinking. This list clearly includes writers such as Dick Beatty, Michael Beer, John Boudreau, Peter Cappelli, Wayne Cascio, Ram Charan, Lee Dyer, Bob Eichinger, Jac Fitz-enz, Fred Foulkes, Bob Gandossy, Jay Galbaith, Marshall Goldsmith, Boris Groysberg, Lynda Gratton, Mark Huselid, Bill Joyce, Tom Kochan, Steve Kerr, Dale Lake, Ed Lawler, Mike Losey, Sue Meisinger, Henry Mintzberg, Jeffrey Pfeffer, Bonner Ritchie, Libby Sartain, Warren Wilhelm, and Patrick Wright.

Additionally, we have been privileged to work in conjunction with The RBL Group (www.rbl.net), which has sponsored this work and offered extensive insights into its implications while proving these ideas in companies around the globe. We are particularly indebted to Norm Smallwood, Managing Partner, and Eric Denna, COO, who keep us all pointed in the right direction. Thanks, of course, to our valued colleagues at RBL past and present without whom this work would not be possible: Allan Freed, Bonner Ritchie, Dave Hanna, David Gilliland, Debbie Ashby, Erin Burns, Ernesto Usher, Gene Dalton, Ginger Bitter, Judy Seegmiller, Justin Britton, Kate Sweetman, Kaylene Allsop, Luke Ellsworth, Meggan Pingree, Melanie Ulrich, Nate Thompson, Paul Thompson, Ryan Lusvardi, Scott Harper, Tricia Smallwood, and Wes Hackett.

Most importantly, a very large thanks to our families who tolerate our writing obsession: Wendy Ulrich, Emily Allen, Nancy Brockbank, Carolyn Younger, and Shari Nyman.

We hope that the guidance and examples found in this book serve to improve HR leaders' ability to add significant value to their organizations.

PREFACE

The bar has been raised on human resources.

In the last 50 years, HR professionals have moved from industrial relations where they negotiate the terms and conditions of work to personnel specialists who have expertise in HR practices like recruiting, compensation, training, and organizational development to business partners who deliver value to business success. We have been privileged to observe and in some cases influence this transition. In the 1990s, we wrote *Human Resource Champions* where we encouraged HR professionals to focus on outcomes more than activities and defined four roles that reflected the outcomes they should deliver (administrative expert, employee champion, strategic partner, and change agent). We evolved these ideas in *HR Value Proposition* by focusing on the creation of value to employees and line managers inside and customers and investors outside the company. We researched and documented the competencies required for HR professionals in *HR Competencies*. In each of these books as well as in dozens of articles and hundreds of workshops, we have learned that HR's more strategic role is much less about having "a seat at the table" than it is about business leaders managing talent and organization issues to reach business goals. When HR professionals help business leaders deliver value to investors, customers, and communities, HR in turn creates value.

As business challenges become more complex with economic, global, technological, competitive, customer, and demographic changes and pressures, business leaders seek innovative solutions to managing short- and long-term cost and growth, both locally and globally. For HR professionals to contribute to these demands, they must transform how they work. This fundamental transformation must occur in the way the HR department is organized (into service centers, centers of expertise, embedded HR); how HR practices are designed, integrated, and aligned to business requirements;

and how HR professionals must be prepared so that they can contribute. The urgency to transform HR is only heightened by an increasingly uncertain economic environment.

The RBL Institute

Throughout our thinking, writing, and consulting on these issues, we continue to learn a great amount from thoughtful and innovative HR leaders. We formalized our learning opportunities when The RBL Group, our consulting firm, founded The RBL Institute, a forum dedicated to helping senior HR executives of member companies create value by advancing the field of strategic HR. Through interactive think tank sessions with leading HR practitioners and thinkers, we link emerging theory with practical solutions that can be immediately applied to create lasting, meaningful results. On frequent calls with the most senior HR leaders in the world, we explore new frameworks for addressing the most pressing problems and identify new venues to test best practices. We then circulate our thoughts with white papers, many of which have been seeds for this work. Finally, we arm our Institute members with tools, processes, and training as they continue to trek through daily quagmires and prove our collective ideas in the trenches. We are honored to learn from thought leaders in leading firms who have taught us by their creation and application of ideas. We feel privileged to work with such a strong group of HR leaders from around the world. Through dialogues with these leading firms and thinkers, we created a series of books about topics critical to the HR profession, including measurement of HR, managing talent, organization redesign, and the like.

Through our discussions with thoughtful HR executives, from our own research, and based on our own experience, we wanted to document how to go about transforming HR. We know the academic theory, have done the empirical research, and have had a number of wonderful consulting engagements. This work is the compilation of our insights: a handbook for HR transformation.

Our Hope for the Future of HR

As observers of the HR profession, we have enormous confidence and hope for the future. In this book, we lay out the pathway for that hope. We suggest the reasons why HR must matter to business leaders and ways in which HR can connect its work inside the organization to customers, investors, and community leaders outside. We define outcomes of good HR work not in terms of activities but organizational capabilities. We offer specific guidelines for transforming HR departments or functions, HR practices, and HR professionals. These guidelines redesign, reengineer, and upgrade the HR profession. We suggest specific roles for line managers, HR professionals, employees, and advisors to deliver on the hope of transformation. We know that we do not have nearly all the answers and that other brilliant colleagues have tackled these problems in slightly different ways. We acknowledge their insights and hope we have complemented their work. By accomplishing transformation, we envision HR continuing to be center stage as organizations face greater business changes than they have ever faced. We are advocates for the profession and the leaders who make it happen. We hope this work and the other books in our series will help continue to make HR the essential source for strategic solutions.

Dave Ulrich
Justin Allen
Wayne Brockbank
Jon Younger
Mark Nyman

I

A HANDBOOK FOR
HR TRANSFORMATION

CHAPTER 1

INTRODUCTION TO HR TRANSFORMATION

1

A few years ago, we sat with a dozen senior human resources executives and academic colleagues, talking about how HR departments should respond to increased expectations given constantly changing and challenging business conditions. We listened as the executives described the business challenges they had faced and how they had transformed the way they work. While our academic colleagues toiled to conceptualize the theory to study their new processes, we realized that we had participated directly or indirectly in the HR transformation with almost all of these executives and with others in a wide range of industries. In many cases, we had experienced firsthand their efforts to contribute to their business. We had helped them discover ways to reshape HR to meet these increased expectations. We had learned with them what worked and what did not work. In short, we had the privilege of working with them to develop the implicit theory, logic, and processes of HR transformation.

Sources (Where This Book Comes From)

This book synthesizes and summarizes the lessons we have learned about HR transformation. We have learned these lessons not in isolation but by working with thoughtful and innovative HR executives who have helped their organizations and the HR profession make meaningful progress in contributing to the performance of their companies. We have learned these lessons both from successes—where the transformation delivered value—and from failures—where we did not make the progress we intended. We hope this book captures both the theory (ideas, rationale, and approaches) and the practices (tools, processes, and actions) for creating a successful HR transformation. Transformation theory draws from change literatures found in sociology, psychology, anthropology, organizational development, systems theory, high-performing teams, and economics. These disciplines teach ways to approach both large-scale and personal change. Transformation theory and practice come as we have applied these ideas in dozens of organizations. Theory without practice is conjecture and is usually irrelevant. Practice without theory is idiosyncratic and unsustainable. We hope to combine theory and practice so that those charged with and affected by HR transformation can make sustainable progress.

Audience (Who Should Read This)

HR professionals: The ideas and tools in this book are targeted primarily to HR professionals. Senior human resources executives face increased accountability for making sure that HR practices and functions align with and drive business results. To fulfill their HR leadership role, they need to be active participants in the process of setting business strategy. They can then set direction for transformation, design a process that focuses on HR results, engage people in the process, execute to ensure transformation happens, and make sure it endures. HR professionals should also be aware of the principles of HR transformation. HR professionals who continually complain about lack of access to business leaders will never gain access. In contrast, HR professionals who understand the transformation principles we present and then implement them will be in a much better position to add significant value.

Line managers: A second important audience for this book is line managers. We find increasing numbers of line managers who believe that issues like talent, organizational capability development, strategy execution, and leadership are the keys to their business success. They increasingly look to HR for thought leadership, insightful recommendations, and practical processes for these issues. If and when they understand the principles of HR transformation, they can be more confident that HR will add value to business success and help them reach their goals.

Staff functions: A third audience for this book is made up of professionals and leaders of other staff functions, including information technology, finance, and legal, who, like HR, are challenged to deliver value. We are finding that principles of HR transformation can readily be adapted to these functions so that these professionals can also successfully transform current processes and practices to help their business meet the challenges in an increasingly difficult environment.

Perspective (Why Our Approach Is Different)

A successful HR transformation increases the value human resources adds to the business. This is a simple statement and one that is easy to gloss over, but it reflects an approach to transformation that is not always practiced. In workshops with HR professionals, we often begin with the general question, "What is the biggest challenge you face in your job today?" As we go around the room, the challenges range from doing HR practices better (hiring people, training leaders, building incentive compensation) to relating to business leaders (having a voice at the table, getting buy-in) to managing the increased personal demands of the HR job (managing time, feeling overwhelmed with so much to do). As heads nod in affirmation of the inevitable and obvious challenges facing HR professionals, we then say that these answers are wrong. Silence ensues.

Simply stated, we propose that the biggest challenge for HR professionals today is to help their respective organizations succeed.

In businesses, promoting success may mean reducing costs, increasing market share, growing in global markets, or innovating new products or services. In government agencies or nonprofit organizations, it may mean delivering services, achieving externally imposed goals, meeting constituent needs, or operating with reduced budgets. Our point is that HR professionals often focus internally on the function of HR rather than externally on what customers and investors need HR to deliver. If HR professionals are to truly serve as business partners, then their goals must be the goals of the business. Transforming HR professionals into business partners isn't an end in and of itself; it's the *means* to a strategic, business-oriented end. Granted, the activities of HR are important—we do recognize that when we say focusing on these HR activities is wrong, we overstate the position to make a point.

Our point is that HR should begin from the outside in. We should be at least as worried about the outcomes of our activities as about the activities themselves. Thus, we ask people to add two simple words—*so that*—to their biggest challenge at work. The "so that" query shifts from a focus on what we do to what we deliver, from the activities we perform to the value that these activities create.

Likewise, an HR transformation should begin with a clear understanding of the business context because the setting in which you do business offers the rationale for the HR transformation you will do. Basic supply-demand logic asserts that if supply is high for any given product or service but demand is zero, then its value is zero. If what we do on the inside does not create value on the outside, in the ability of the company to attract, serve, and retain customers and investors, its value is zero.

This logic has many practical implications. For example, many HR leaders launching an HR transformation have an all-hands meeting to share the vision and goals of the new HR organization. We strongly suggest that this event begin with a detailed discussion about the business. In one case, a new head of HR in the airline industry spent the first two hours reviewing fuel costs, load factors, customer satisfaction indexes, regulatory changes, equipment age, and competitive positioning. As we sat in the back of the room, we heard a number of HR professionals whispering to each other, "When are we going to get to HR?" In fact, he was defining the agenda for HR transformation by focusing on the business first. In monthly staff meetings, in performance reviews, and in casual hallway conversations, when we begin our business conversations by talking about the business, it sends a message: HR transformation is not about doing HR; it is about building business success.

Common Pitfalls (Derailers to Watch Out For)

With our focus on business success in mind, it is easier to see some predictable and common mistakes often made when starting an HR transformation:

- *Action before rationale.* Some companies begin an HR transformation by doing things in human resources such as implementing e-HR, restructuring the HR function, or designing new HR practices. These HR investments are then defined as transformational. If these actions are not tied to a business rationale and rooted in the business context, however, they are not transformational and are unlikely to be sustained. HR transformation needs to be grounded in the context of business demands.
- *HR in isolation.* At one company, we worked with HR leaders who had set aside time in July (because this was a slower time for HR) and drafted a strategy about what the HR department was doing and which HR practices would be developed. Meanwhile, the line managers drafted their business strategy in the fall to focus attention on the next year. The result was painful misalignment. When an HR strategy is drafted in isolation from the business strategy, both suffer as stand-alone documents that probably won't be sustained. HR transformation needs to be aligned with business transformation. It needs to be done in a way that focuses on adding value to the business rather than simply optimizing HR as a function.
- *HR in increments.* Some companies design an innovative talent management, performance management, or total rewards process and declare it an HR transformation. These piecemeal efforts are only part of an HR transformation. HR practices need to be integrated with each other around key business results if they are to have lasting value.
- *HR by individual fiat.* Some companies invest in an HR transformation because of the whims of an individual leader or a desire for more personal or functional influence. These individually sponsored initiatives probably won't be transformational. HR transformation needs to be connected to the overall success of the organization, not just an individual champion.

- *Placing HR structure before business strategy.* Occasionally HR departments believe that reorganizing human resources is the essence of HR transformation. They may spend considerable time establishing service centers and centers of expertise or hiring a league of HR business partners, and then declare that they have transformed HR. HR transformation can only be complete as it helps implement the business strategy and drives business results.
- *Efficiency equals transformation.* We are finding more and more HR departments that equate efficiency improvements with HR transformation; for example, a major global pharmaceutical company recently announced that its creation of a shared service center constituted transformation. A leading consumer products company described self-service as its HR transformation. Efficiency improvements can and usually are key elements of transformation, but efficiency alone does not make for transformational change.

We call these derailers viruses, because they infect and can cripple the process of transformation. When identified and confronted, they can be treated and overcome.

TOOL 1.1	*Full Virus List*
	In our work on managing change, we have identified more than 30 common viruses—common reasons why change does not proceed as intended. Download the full list of organizational viruses and learn more about virus busting.
	▶ *Go to www.TransformHR.com*

Our Definition of HR Transformation

A true HR transformation is an integrated, aligned, innovative, and business-focused approach to redefining how HR work is done within an organization so that it helps the organization deliver on promises made to customers, investors, and other stakeholders. This work begins by being very clear about the rationale for doing HR transformation. The rationale for HR transformation is too often from inside the company (say, when a senior leader complains about HR practices, structure, or people), whereas the rationale should actually come from outside the company.

A Model for Transforming HR

We propose a four-phase model for HR transformation to ensure that HR drives business success and avoids the common pitfalls of such efforts. This model (see Figure 1.1) addresses four simple questions about HR transformation:

- Phase 1: Build the business case. (Why do transformation?) HR transformation begins with a clear rationale for why transformation matters. This is addressed in Chapter 2, in terms of knowing the business context and building a case for change.
- Phase 2: Define the outcomes. (What are the outcomes of transformation?) This phase clarifies the expected outcomes from the transformation. What should happen because we invest in HR transformation? Answers to this question are addressed in Chapter 3, which defines the outcomes of HR transformation as the capabilities of a firm or the intangibles that an investor values.
- Phase 3: Redesign HR. (How do we do HR transformation?) HR transformation requires change in HR strategy around departments, practices, and people. Chapters 4, 5, and 6 focus on how to change HR departments, people, and practices.
- Phase 4: Engage line managers and others. (Who should be part of the HR transformation?) HR transformation requires that many people participate in defining and delivering the transformation. Who is involved is discussed in Chapter 7. This chapter focuses on transferring ownership to line management and on strategies for building HR's capability to create sustained change.

Finally, in Chapter 8, we summarize these phases with a set of milestones, each with outcomes and activities that can be performed to successfully accomplish transformation.

While we list these four phases sequentially, in reality they occur concurrently. For example, while knowledge of business conditions has to frame HR transformation (phase 1), having the right HR transformation team (phase 4) is critical to initiating HR transformation. The formation of the HR transformation team is critical to the entire process.

Figure 1.1 Model for HR Transformation

Our recommendation in using this model is that it needs to be adapted, not adopted. We believe that the issues raised in each of the four steps are important and should be considered in ways that make sense for your organization. It is clearly dangerous to simply adopt a model, regardless of its source, whether a successful competitor, an academic, or a consultant, rather than to adapt it. How would you tailor these steps to your situation? How would you cook a meal that works for you? How would you improvise based on the recipe? This book offers some recipes for HR transformation. To make HR transformation work in your organization, you will have to adapt these ingredients and improvise your own original HR transformation recipe. Chapter 8 suggests how to go about doing the transformation.

To flesh out the principles and tools for HR transformation, we have divided the book into two parts. In Part I, we propose the four-step HR Transformation Model and present principles and tools for how to design and deliver a HR transformation.

Part II includes four case studies from organizations that have recently embarked on transformation journeys. They provide examples of how they have combined different transformation ingredients to achieve results that have had an impact in their organizations. Chapter 9 presents HR transformation at Flextronics; Chapter 10 discusses Pfizer; Chapter 11, Intel; and Chapter 12, Takeda. We are grateful to these organizations for their willingness to share their experiences and knowledge with us all.

We hope these case studies help enliven the theories and steps we outline in Part I and give readers a sense of the possibilities they can achieve in their own organizations.

Tools for Transformation

In keeping with the goals of the HR Leadership Series, we provide a toolbox in the Appendix to support you as you design and deliver your organization's

HR transformation journey. We also provide a short, carefully selected list of books and articles that may prove helpful to you or your transformation team in designing the transformation. You'll also find biographies of all the contributors who have helped make this book a success.

TOOL 1.2	*HR Transformation Model Overview*
▶	Watch a video of Dave Ulrich introducing the HR transformation model. Learn as he grounds this theory in reality with examples of how companies have implemented each phase of the model.
	▶ *Go to www.TransformHR.com*

Phase 1:

BUSINESS CONTEXT

CHAPTER 2

WHY DO THE
TRANSFORMATION?

2

When people understand the why of change they are more likely to accept the what. This simple principle is taught by a broad range of change specialists, from the most academic of cognitive psychologists to the most popular of self-help gurus. It holds true not only in personal change (exercise, weight loss, anger management) but also in HR transformation. For personal change, for example, when we fully grasp why we should change a personal behavior, we are more likely to change what we do. The context of a business setting captures the "why" of HR transformation. When HR transformation connects to the context of the business, it is more likely to be sustained because it responds to real needs. This means linking HR efforts directly to the business strategy and to the environmental factors that frame the strategy.

Therefore, we begin by reviewing business conditions and stakeholder expectations. Before jumping in, however, identify your level of readiness for HR transformation by completing the assessment that begins on the following page.

TOOL 2.1 *HR Strategy Assessment*

How often is each of the following statements true in your organization?	1=almost never, 3=sometimes, 5=almost always

How often is each of the following statements true in your organization?

Phase 1: Business Case for Transformation (Chapter 2)

1. All HR professionals have a strong understanding of the business, our competitors, and the external business environment. ① ② ③ ④ ⑤

2. We take an outside-in approach to HR work priorities based on external stakeholder (customer, investor, regulator, etc.) expectations. ① ② ③ ④ ⑤

Phase 2: Define the Outcomes (Chapter 3)

3. Our organization has clearly defined organizational capabilities that ensure strategy execution. ① ② ③ ④ ⑤

4. HR leaders focus on business results (by delivering organizational capabilities), not activities. ① ② ③ ④ ⑤

5. HR measurably contributes to the investor intangible value and customer brand reputation of the organization. ① ② ③ ④ ⑤

Phase 3a: HR Department Design (Chapter 4)

6. Our entire HR staff understands our HR strategy and can explain how their work ties to the strategy. ① ② ③ ④ ⑤

7. Our HR organization clearly differentiates transactional and strategic HR work. ① ② ③ ④ ⑤

8. HR is sized correctly (staff, costs) for the requirements of the organization. ① ② ③ ④ ⑤

Phase 3b: HR Practice Design (Chapter 5)

9. We have strong people, performance, information, and work processes that are directly tied to strategic organizational outcomes. ① ② ③ ④ ⑤

10. Our HR processes are effectively integrated, e.g., what we do in talent management is reinforced by our reward practices. ① ② ③ ④ ⑤

11. Overall, our HR processes are effectively aligned to our business strategies. ① ② ③ ④ ⑤

Phase 3c: Upgrade HR Professionals (Chapter 6)

12. We have clearly defined HR competencies, roles, and activities that directly tie to business success. ① ② ③ ④ ⑤

13. We do a good job of assessing HR professionals against competencies needed to deliver business success.   ① ② ③ ④ ⑤

14. We actively invest in our HR professionals and tie our development investments to business outcomes.   ① ② ③ ④ ⑤

Phase 4: Engage Line Managers and Others (Chapter 7)

15. Our people and organizational initiatives are led by line managers and enabled by HR.   ① ② ③ ④ ⑤

16. HR helps gather customer insights and ensures that the organization is designed to deliver on promises made to customers.   ① ② ③ ④ ⑤

17. HR leaders understand investor needs and clearly align initiatives to deliver value for investors.   ① ② ③ ④ ⑤

If your score is greater than 80, you have already transformed your HR organization to a large extent. Congratulations! Use this book to identify ways to continuously improve.

If your score is between 50 and 80, you have a significant opportunity to improve HR contribution through a focused and well-organized transformation effort. Use this book to build and implement your plan.

If your score is below 50, it is important that you begin work on your HR transformation immediately. Use this book to build and implement your plan.

TOOL 2.2	*Preparing for HR Transformation*
	Learn from Jon Younger as he describes how to create the conditions you need to initiate a successful HR transformation and shares best practices in HR transformation preparation. Share this video with your team during your transformation kick-off meeting.
	▶ *Go to www.TransformHR.com*

TOOL 2.3	*HR Transformation Jumpstart Methods*
	Download additional ideas and approaches when launching an HR transformation initiative.
	▶ *Go to www.TransformHR.com*

Understand General Business Conditions and Specific Stakeholders' Expectations

While we are staunch advocates of aligning human resources with business strategy, we recommend that HR leaders not only look at the business strategy but also look *through* the strategy to see and understand the business conditions or external realities that shape it. Traditional strategy is like a mirror where HR can reflect its investment. We recommend looking through the mirror (strategy) to external customers and investors to fully understand the antecedents of the strategy. Understanding and linking HR with these contextual constituents helps HR not just implement the strategy but play a key role in defining it. By focusing on the business context, HR can avoid the common mistake of seeking to implement internally focused ideas and concepts that come across as solutions looking for problems. To build this rationale for doing HR transformation, you need to understand general business conditions and specific stakeholders' expectations, and then use that understanding to build a business case for the transformation.

General Business Conditions

Most of us are at least casually aware of general business conditions, especially with the world facing economic difficulties worse than those seen for several decades. Some of these business conditions are cyclical as industries go through inevitable cycles of growth and retraction. Other conditions are more structural and include fundamental changes in globalization, technology, demographics, and the political landscape. General economic trends like unemployment, inflation, exchange rates, balance of trade, investor confidence, and overextended credit create both economic cycles and structural changes in an industry, both of which affect HR investments and management strategy.

Globalization has made the world "flat"—a global village with new markets offering new challenges and opportunities. At the same time, business in mature markets differs from business in developing markets like Brazil, Russia, India, and China and differs even more from what is needed for so-called emerging markets in sub-Saharan Africa, the Middle East, Southeast Asia, and Latin America. These markets have divergent economic cycles, with most growing while others shrink. Global issues also deal with sourcing commodities and issues such as volatile energy costs, trade barriers, exchange rates, tariffs, and distribution. Technology has increased accessibility, visibility, and connectivity. The connected world is smaller, is rapidly changing, and has more open information. Technology obsolescence occurs ever more quickly as the half-life of knowledge shrinks. Demographic trends require that workplaces be able to respond not only to current employees but to future employees and customers. Creating a workforce that adapts to gender, generational, and ethnic differences helps organizations survive over time. And political uncertainty may hinder investment because of the lack of confidence in social stability. Political shifts affect not only consumer confidence but organizational opportunities and challenges.

These and other general business conditions have indirect yet real effects on how business strategies are formed and delivered. And as Anita McGahan and Michael Porter discuss, others have shown that these general business conditions account for about 50 percent of organizational performance. These conditions are outside the control of any one leader and yet shape the context in which work is done.

HR professionals who want to contribute to strategy formulation and to sustain a transformation should be more than casual observers of these trends. It is not necessary to be an economist, demographer, or political scientist to do HR transformation, but it is important to be conversant in these fields. Learning these general business conditions means more than offhand reading of newspapers or Internet news stories and watching television. It means really understanding who customers are and why they buy, why investors choose to invest or withhold funds, how markets work, as well as the demographic trends in critical markets, the technological forces facing your organization, and the political choices that might affect your organization.

This means meeting with experts inside your company and asking them probing questions, reading articles and books that help you understand current business conditions, and attending workshops where these issues are discussed. We recommend that HR professionals spend an hour or two a week reading and doing basic Internet-based research on the broad factors shaping the economy and their industry.

In addition to personal research and self-education, we also find that HR departments with a transformative bent are excellent at providing tools and processes to keep the entire team in touch with basic business conditions. For example, in Chapter 1, we told the story of the head of HR in a global airline spending time with his HR team talking about airline industry trends. Kellogg HR starts quarterly global HR leadership team meetings with a review of fundamental business performance and what's happening in the broader market. The HR team of Saint Gobain in Asia Pacific shares fundamental business intelligence from across its markets—from China to Australia.

Specific Stakeholder Expectations

More directly, business context can be defined in terms of specific stakeholders your organization must respond to. When we talk to HR groups, we often ask, "Who are your customers?" Inevitably, 70 to 80 percent respond that employees are the customers of HR and that HR should build practices to increase employee competence and commitment. That makes sense, but it's only partially correct. While we agree that employees are critical stakeholders of HR's work, they are not the only stakeholders. A more complete model of HR includes multiple stakeholders—employees and line managers inside the organization, and customers, investors, regulators, competitors, and communities outside the organization. To fully grasp business conditions specific to your organization and HR transformation, you must identify particular expectations and changes for each of these stakeholders. General business conditions become more focused when they translate into specific expectations of key stakeholders.

Employees

Employee demographics have a significant impact on work. Employees represent increasingly diverse backgrounds, with diversity including not only race and gender but personal preferences, global or cultural roots, cognitive style, age, and orientation to work. In your work in HR, you should study your organization's internal and external demographics. Internally, look for demographic patterns to see if employee differences are nurtured, encouraged, and leveraged. Prepare your managers to encourage high performance from people who are different from themselves, and encourage them to surround themselves with people who, although different from themselves, are just as committed to company and personal performance. Externally, learn the demographic trends that affect how you will source talent in the future. Invest, for example, in the quality of education for future employees either in your local education systems or in specialized job requirements for your company. Explore alternative sources of talent (for example, hiring older or retired employees part-time, building relationships with universities outside your home markets, or using technology to access talent from distant countries). Build policies and practices inside your company that respond to demographic changes (for example, by helping employees use technology to stay connected to their work and to friendship groups).

Line Managers

Line managers charged with defining and executing strategy to deliver results constitute a key stakeholder group for HR transformation. A decade ago, HR professionals were clamoring to "be at the table" when key business decisions were made. Today, most competent HR professionals have access to business discussions. In seminars, we ask, "How many of you could have 30 minutes with your general manager in the next week if you asked for it?" Ninety percent say they have access.

So HR is at the table. Now the great challenge looms: What do we contribute?

If, in business discussions, HR professionals wait for "HR issues" to come up (number and types of people required for a business goal, type of compensation system, improved organization design), they will likely wait beyond their welcome. Any number of functions want space and time at the table; only those who add value are invited to keep attending. With line managers facing ever-increasing scrutiny and pressures and CEO tenure declining, HR professionals should be active contributors in business discussions, not just HR discussions. This requires thinking about the business through the eyes of your line manager: What is that manager accountable for? What's on the scorecard? What topics come to mind first? What are the problems that cannot easily be solved? Anticipating and working on these problems helps you as an HR professional deliver value. Additionally, contributing HR professionals have their own opinions concerning the future strategy of the business and often share their views with their line managers.

Customers

Customers have become increasingly segmented, literate, and demanding. As they are offered greater choice, they become more selective about choosing organizations to work with. Your job in HR is to identify your target customers and find out why they do business with your organization and how you can begin to build or rebuild relationships with former customers. HR professionals who spend time learning about and working with customers have a clear line of sight between HR practices and customer share. We suggest that HR professionals should spend about a day a quarter joining sales representatives in customer calls. When visiting customers, HR professionals should focus on the value they can provide customers rather than simply approaching the meeting as a developmental opportunity for their own growth.

While sales personnel sometimes focus on selling a particular product or service, HR professionals can focus on building relationships. Human resources is in a unique position to help build long-term relationships with customers by demonstrating that their company has both the organizational capability and the talent in place to deliver on the sales team's promises. Customers who know that you are going to hire, train, pay, and organize work to meet their needs will be more likely to form an enduring relationship with you. Obtaining customer insights by reviewing marketing data and knowing specific customers by spending time with them makes you aware of how HR investments link to these customer needs.

Investors

Investors have become increasingly attuned to and actively concerned about intangibles as well as financial results. Capital markets have shifted. Activist owners in hedge funds, sovereign wealth funds, or other major shareholders will increasingly look beyond the balance sheet and into the quality of leadership and organization that give them confidence in the future. HR professionals who know the goals of the company's investors (growth versus value; short-term versus long-term) can more carefully craft HR practices that will give these investors confidence in the future. Intangibles now account for a significant portion of total shareholder return, and HR professionals should have a point of view about how to define and enhance intangible value. HR professionals can participate in meetings to learn investor expectations and can function as presenters to help investors have confidence in future success. In *How Leaders Build Value*, we argue that critical steps to creating intangible value include keeping promises, ensuring a compelling strategy, aligning core competencies, and aligning organizational capabilities. We call this the "Architecture for Intangibles" and show four intangible factors that HR professionals should master: meeting current commitments, clarifying future strategy, developing core competencies, and building organizational capabilities.

Competitors

Competition comes both from traditional, large global players as well as from smaller innovators. The rate of global growth continues, but increasingly that growth is coming from emerging markets. Knowing present and future competitors requires insight into how industries will shift and evolve on a global as well as a local scale. Mapping current and future competitors, reviewing their strengths and weaknesses, and plotting your strategies to outperform them helps you shape HR practices that will differentiate your organization. HR professionals can also lead in benchmarking competitors' organizational capabilities in talent, speed to market, innovation, customer service, efficiency, and leadership as a way to signal market threats or opportunities.

Global Suppliers

Suppliers connected to the firm become a source of advantage or disadvantage. Supplier management reduces risks and ensures continuity of service. Just as HR can connect staffing, training, and compensation with customers, it can do so with suppliers to ensure stability of operations. HR should be able to assess and help leverage individual talent and organizational capabilities at every phase of the integrated value chain. Furthermore, HR insights can help develop ways to stabilize critical resources by forming stable and cost-effective supply contracts.

Regulators

Government agencies may define policy that favors or hinders your business. As political trends shift from more to less and back to more regulation, you should be aware of how those trends will affect your organization's ability not only to attract talent but to compete in new markets. Regulations increasingly focus on processes used to govern (Sarbanes-Oxley, for example), and HR executives can be activists in anticipating and responding to legislation. While local and national regulations continue to increase, also be aware that many trade tariffs continue to drop, prompting greater global competition and the mandate to create more competitive corporate cultures at every organizational level.

Community

Reputation also becomes important as your organization's social standing becomes part of its success. Increasingly, companies are being judged by a triple bottom line, and they are encouraged to invest in sustainability and manage their carbon use, to engage in philanthropy by giving back to the communities in which they operate, and to build the employability of their workforce as they create jobs for the local population and work practices that treat employees well. HR professionals can be leaders in shaping socially responsible practices that help the organization gain a strong reputation for attracting talent, customers, and capital.

Addressing Stakeholders

As organizations position themselves with each of these stakeholders, HR professionals should shape unique strategies to compete over time. Knowing who the stakeholders are for your company and advocating how to deal with them will ensure that you align HR transformation with issues that matter. The purpose of HR transformation is to ensure that stakeholders receive value from your company. Creating a clear line of sight between your HR transformation and your stakeholders will help you build the business case for transformation. To reiterate, HR transformation is not just about what you do within HR; it is about the value for key stakeholders that your actions will create.

These general business conditions and the requirements of specific stakeholders shape an organization's strategy, and they also define why you should do an HR transformation. HR's historical legacy has been to monitor terms and conditions of work through industrial relations, then to design systems and practices that shape how people are treated in an organization. With this orientation, HR professionals had little reason to be more than casual observers of general business trends or specific stakeholder expectations. Current and future generations of human resources will design and implement HR transformations that should link HR efforts with business strategies to position the organization in its business context. Figure 2.1 outlines the model that we suggest.

Figure 2.1 *Traditional Versus Transformative HR*

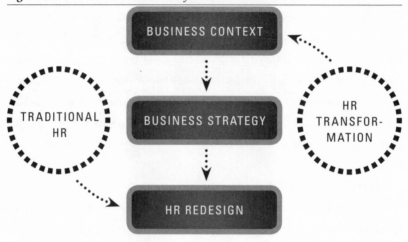

Traditional HR begins by focusing on HR issues and redesigning HR governance or practices. HR transformation begins with an understanding of the context in which the business operates (both general conditions and specific stakeholders). This context provides the rationale for why HR transformation should occur.

TOOL 2.4	*Stakeholder Analysis*
	Be very clear to ensure your stakeholders' expectations and needs are addressed at the beginning and are embedded in everything you do throughout the HR transformation. Download and print the Stakeholder Analysis Worksheets. Have your entire team complete the worksheet, then prioritize stakeholder needs.
	▶ *Go to www.TransformHR.com*

TOOL 2.5	*External Environment*
	Understanding the complexities in your external environment is critical to a sustainable HR transformation. Watch Wayne Brockbank explain the impact of external environment on successful transformation.
	▶ *Go to www.TransformHR.com*

Build a Business Case for HR Transformation

As we said in the first chapter, many HR professionals define their biggest challenge as doing HR work better. HR professionals often see their largest job challenges as sourcing talent, improving performance management, defining compensation, and providing training programs and other HR systems. *We suggest that real HR transformation begins by responding to the general business conditions and specifically serving key stakeholders.* When HR professionals start by thinking about the outcomes of their work as defined by the business context, they change their conversations with line managers and are better able to justify why an HR transformation should occur.

The implications of this approach show up in the meeting when HR transformation is being proposed. In this meeting, either with a line manager or a senior executive team, the inevitable question will arise: Why are we doing this transformation work? As noted, many HR leaders will answer from an internal perspective: to build better talent, rewards, structure, or communication practices. When these outcomes are linked to the business context, however, the justification for the HR transformation is stronger. The following cases illustrate the business case for HR transformation:

- *Example 1:* Our competitors have produced 30 percent more revenue from products introduced in the last three years than we have, and we think that this is one reason their price/earnings ratios and market value have been higher than ours. We believe that if we transform HR, we will be able to move more quickly in acquiring the right talent and creating the right orga-nization to produce more innovative products and to build a better reputa-tion within the capital markets.

- *Example 2:* We see a large portion of our future growth coming from emerg-ing markets. Our estimate is that traditional North American and European markets for our products have slowed while Asian and Middle Eastern mar-kets are expanding rapidly. We need to transform our HR processes for tal-ent, performance, and communication to prepare us to enter these markets more quickly than our competitors—who recognize the same trends. HR should give us a first- and fast-mover advantage in developing and deliver-ing this global strategy.

- *Example 3:* Our customer base is dramatically changing. While we once could rely on long-term social connections to secure customers, we are finding that prospects are using more rigorous financial criteria and are more willing to select suppliers on the basis of cost. With new competitors from China and India being able to exploit a cost advantage, we need to transform HR in order to find ways to increase labor productivity while concurrently changing our culture to meet these customer challenges and competitor responses.

- *Example 4:* The newly elected government is likely to change the rules for our industry. We will probably get smaller subsidies for our R&D and less tax relief. We need to prepare our people and organization to respond to these changes. We need to change our HR approach to adapt to these legis-lative trends.

- *Example 5:* The labor pool for the markets where we need to compete in the future is shrinking, particularly in specialized positions where we are in a real war for talent. For us to pursue an innovation strategy, we must contin-ually source the top talent in our specific targeted areas. We are finding that our retention of top talent in key positions is worse than our competitors' and puts us at competitive risk. We need to transform HR practices so that we can source, retain, and leverage top talent.

- *Example 6:* The age of our workforce is a real concern. Because of past hir-ing practices, 40 percent of our senior technical and managerial talent are eligible to retire in the next four years. If they choose to do so, this will create an enormous knowledge gap. We need to quickly transform HR practices around retirement to secure knowledge for our future and develop staffing practices to stabilize our workforce.

- *Example 7:* We have grown quickly in the last few years, and 70 percent of our employees have been with us less than five years. The embedded culture that shaped this company is no longer implicitly shared with these new hires. They have enormous technical talent, but we need to make sure they also reflect the values of the company. HR transformation will help more quickly transfer our heritage to the new employees and at the same time enable them to teach our mature employees about new opportunities they may not have seen. We don't want to outgrow our talent.

- *Example 8:* We have lost more than our share of recent competitive bids to our competition. In analyzing why we have lost, we realize that we have been too slow to respond to customer queries, unable to tailor our product and service offerings, and too complex to do business with. We believe that an HR transformation will help us streamline our organization so that we achieve a higher success rate in winning competitive bids.

These types of discussions take many HR people out of their traditional comfort zones. They must learn to understand and diagnose business context settings as business leaders. They need to grasp general economic conditions, specific industry trends, customer and competitor moves, and regulatory and technological environments. They need to position HR transformation as a response to real and future business problems. They need to use data about external realities and not intuition to justify the transformation. They need to partner with marketing, finance, and other staff groups to obtain data that will inform the rationale for seeking transformation.

In addition, in building the rationale for transformation, they will want to pay attention to the risks of not doing it. If the transformation does not occur, what will happen to their ability to respond to general business conditions and key stakeholder expectations? They will also want to recognize how HR transformation fits with other initiatives in the company. This means building the case for HR transformation as a priority in the midst of other competing demands.

Conclusion

For change to lead to sustained transformation, you need to present a business case that justifies the investment. We believe that when the presenting problem for HR transformation comes from the context of the business and from the expectations of key stakeholders, then the case for transformation is stronger than if the presenting problem originates primarily inside the business.

TOOL 2.6	*Business Case Worksheet*
	Download a copy of the business case worksheet. Encourage each member of the HR transformation team to complete the worksheet prior to your business case development meeting.
	▶ *Go to www.TransformHR.com*

TOOL 2.7	*HR Transformation Business Case*
	Watch Justin Allen describe a process for developing a transformation business case and listen as he shares examples of transformation teams who have successfully communicated their business case to the Board of Directors, the senior executive team, the HR leadership team, and HR professionals throughout the organization.
	▶ *Go to www.TransformHR.com*

Phase 2:
OUTCOMES

CHAPTER 3

WHAT ARE THE OUTCOMES OF THE HR TRANSFORMATION?

3

HR transformation is not a single event—it's a new pattern of thought and behavior. As discussed in Chapter 2, the rationale for the transformation comes from general business conditions and the ability to increase value to specific stakeholders. Once business leaders acknowledge that HR transformation will help them respond to business challenges, they will inevitably want to know how to measure the impact of the transformation.

The traditional answer is that you can measure specific quantitative outcomes of HR practices. For example:

- How many people did we hire?
- What percentage of low performers was removed from the organization?
- How many employees completed the required 20 or 40 hours of training in the past year?
- How many information sessions were held?

But if that's all you do, it is not enough. It is not unimportant to measure the activity of human resources, but you also need to measure the outcome or value of these activities. Tracking activity is not the same as tracking fundamental transformation or increased value creation.

We suggest that HR transformation has two types of outcomes. First, the stakeholder expectations identified in Chapter 2 should be realized. HR transformation should play a significant part in determining stakeholder results. Second, HR transformation can be tracked by the capabilities an organization creates.

Stakeholder Measures

In Chapter 2, we suggested that part of specifying your organization's context is to define and deliver value to stakeholders inside and outside the company. This stakeholder mapping helps you build the case for why HR transformation is important. It also provides the basis for measuring results. Having specified a line of sight between HR activities and value delivered to key stakeholders, you then need to come up with clear and simple measures to track the extent of the benefit positive changes provide key stakeholders. If the HR transformation is successful, then a number of outcomes can and should occur for each stakeholder.

In Table 3.1, we summarize some of these outcomes. In building your HR transformation plan, you may want to pick the stakeholders you are most worried about and then discuss and define the outcomes that will be most important for them. These outcomes should be operationally defined, measured, and tracked over time to quantify the progress of your HR transformation. The process of clarifying stakeholders and outcomes will come from your HR transformation advisory team as they respond to the following questions:

- If we are to divide 100 points among the possible stakeholders who are most important for future business success and who will receive value from our HR transformation, how will we divide these points? Your team should come to a shared perspective on weighting which stakeholders (employees, line managers, customers, regulators, investors, communities) matter most and will be most affected by the transformation.
- For the stakeholders who matter most, what measures are reliable, accurate, transparent, and easy to collect? For each key stakeholder, your team should select the two or three key indicators for tracking progress of the transformation.
- How will you collect the data so that you can benchmark where you are today and track where you are going in the future? You need to build a systematic process for collecting, sharing, and monitoring the data of your stakeholder

Table 3.1 Measures of Key Stakeholders from HR Transformation

STAKEHOLDER	POSSIBLE MEASURES
Employees	• Greater competence for present and future jobs • More engagement or commitment • Higher productivity • Increased retention of talented employees • Willingness to refer company to other potential hires
Leaders and Leadership	• Measure of backup talent (number of qualified people for key jobs) • Able to export talent to the rest of the company • Able to do an organization diagnosis and identify key capabilities • Shared focus on what the strategy is • Help make strategy happen • Seen by associates (for example in a 360-degree feedback exercise) as demonstrating competencies required for a leader
Customers	• More customer share of targeted customers (share of wallet) • More loyalty and satisfaction with the firm on customer surveys • Greater willingness to engage in long-term relationship with the firm • Willingness to recommend firm to others • Percentage of new projects won from competitive bidding
Regulators	• Trust the firm to do the right things • Give the firm voice in defining regulations • Perceive the firm as one that abides by laws and regulations
Analysts / Investors	• Higher Price to Earnings (market to book) value • Belief in growth strategy • Higher confidence in future earnings • Trust quality of leadership to make the right decisions about strategy, people, customers, and operations
Community	• Receives recognition as employer of choice • Manages environment responsibly (reduces carbon footprint) • Gives back to the community (philanthropy) in terms of money and time • Encourages safe and positive employee work practices • Builds a positive reputation as a good place to work

results. This information will become part of the transformation scorecard and help you monitor how you are doing.

As you follow these steps, you can begin to see the impact of your HR transformation in terms of outcomes as seen by the stakeholders you serve.

Capability Measures

While stakeholder measures track the outcomes of HR transformation as seen by the recipients of the transformation, we believe that the HR transformation should also change the fundamental identity, culture, or image of the company. We refer to this outcome of HR transformation as *defining and building capabilities*. Capabilities shape the way people think about organizations. When we work with executives to define the organization of the future, we ask them a simple question: "Can you name a company you admire?" The list of admired companies varies, but it often includes such well-known firms as General Electric, Apple, Disney, Google, or Microsoft. We then ask, "How many levels of management does the admired firm have?" Almost no one ever knows.

More important, no one really cares—we do not admire an organization because of its roles, rules, or routines. Instead, we admire a company like GE because of its capacity to build leaders in diverse industries; we admire Apple because it seems to continually design easy-to-use products; we admire Disney for the outstanding service we experience; we admire Google and Microsoft for their ability to innovate and shape their industry. In other words, organizations are known not for their *structure* but for their *capabilities*.

Capabilities represent what the organization is known for, what it is good at doing, and how it patterns activities to deliver value. The capabilities define many of the intangibles that investors pay attention to, the firm brand customers can relate to, and the culture that shapes employee behavior. These capabilities also become the identity of the firm, the deliverables of HR practices, and the keys to implementing business strategy. Capabilities can and should be monitored by measuring and tracking them.

TOOL 3.1	*Organizational Capabilities*
	Watch a video of Dave Ulrich explaining the importance of organizational capabilities and why they are HR's number one deliverable.
	▶ *Go to www.TransformHR.com*

TOOL 3.2	*Organizational Capability Assessment*
	Be sure your HR transformation team is clear about the capabilities your organization needs. Check out the RBL Organizational Capability Assessment.
	▶ *Go to www.TransformHR.com*

There is no magic list of desired or ideal capabilities. However, the following capabilities and their measures seem to be inherent in well-managed firms:

Talent

Speed

Shared mind-set

Accountability

Collaboration

Learning

Leadership

Customer connection

Innovation

Strategic unity

Simplicity

Social responsibility

Risk

Efficiency

Talent

We are good at attracting, motivating, and retaining competent and committed people.

Assuring talent means going beyond platitudes such as "people are our most important asset" and "strategy follows people" and investing time and resources to securing superior talent. Employees must be both competent and committed. Competent employees have the skills for today's and tomorrow's business requirements. Committed employees deploy those skills regularly and predictably. Leaders can assess the extent to which their organization regularly attracts and keeps top talent and the extent to which that talent is fully applied for optimal performance. Assuring competent employees comes as leaders buy (bring in new talent), build (develop existing talent), borrow (access thought leaders through alliances or partnerships), bounce (remove poor talent), and bind (keep the best talent).

Competence of employees can be tracked by assessing the percentage of employees who have the skills to do their job today and in the future, by benchmarking current employees against competitors, and by productivity measures that track employee output per unit of employee input. One firm tracks the number of its employees who are targeted by search firms, regarding this as a good thing because it suggests a reservoir of talented employees. Another invites investors to visit and ask any employee any question about the firm's strategy, product, or financial position. This test of business literacy impresses investors, who can thus determine firsthand the competence of employees.

Assuring commitment comes when leaders build an employee value proposition that ensures that employees who contribute more will in turn receive more of what matters most to them. Leaders can track commitment through retention of the top employees. (And lack of retention of the bottom tier; we often suggest that the most strategic human resource decision a company can make is to place its worst performers with its competitors.) Leaders can also track commitment through employee attitude surveys done frequently as pulse checks and by direct observation as executives intuitively sense the engagement level of employees. Leaders who build both competent and committed employees ensure a flow of talent that helps the organization perform well over time.

Speed

We are good at making important changes happen fast.

Gaining speed allows a company to turn a mediocre change ability into a fast, agile change capability. Speed means that the organization can quickly identify and move into new markets, develop and deliver new products or services, solidify new employee contracts, and operationalize new business processes. Leaders embed this capability into the organization by being focused on making decisions rigorously and expeditiously, by implementing change processes throughout their organization, by removing bureaucratic barriers to change, and by eliminating other viruses that inhibit change. Enhancing the capacity to change takes time because the laws of entropy keep change from happening, but when large firms act like small, nimble firms, they master the speed capability.

Speed can be tracked in a variety of ways, all involving time. Time can be tracked from concept to commercialization of an idea, from changeover of an assembly line to the first new product to roll off it, from collecting customer data to market research, from moving products to and through the distribution channels, from the time to scale of production, and from proposing an administrative change to fully implementing that change. Just as increasing inventory turns shows that physical assets are well used, saving time demonstrates both financial savings in terms of labor productivity, but also increased enthusiasm and responsiveness to opportunities ahead of the competition.

Shared Mind-Set

We are good at ensuring that customers and employees have positive images of and experiences with our organization.

Gaining a shared mind-set, or firm brand identity, can be a vital capability. In our view, a shared mind-set is a unity of identity where the external image (brand, reputation) of your organization is consistent with your internal culture. This unity of identity comes from understanding how firms move from individual product brands to firm brands. The Marriott name on a hotel adds value because it gives the traveler confidence in the product. GE emphasizes "Imagination at Work" across a wide array of products and services. Being affiliated with the Olympics brand is worth millions to companies who want to be associated with the positive image of the Olympics tradition. Leaders can identify and shape their shared mind-set, or firm brand, by building a consensus among their management team regarding what they want the firm to be "known for" by its best customers in the future. Once a consensus is reached on this identity, leaders can invest in a series of actions to make the identity real to both customers and employees.

Shared mind-set can be measured with a simple exercise. Ask your team to answer the question: What are the top three things we want to be known for by our best customers in the future? Collect the responses to this query and measure the degree of consensus as the percentage of responses that fall into the most common three categories. We have done this exercise hundreds of times, often to find a shared mind-set in the 50–60 percent range. Leading firms score in the 80–90 percent range because they have a clear sense of what they want to be known for by customers. The next step in the exercise is to invite key customers to answer the same question. That will let you monitor the extent to which the internal and external mind-sets are shared, providing a clear index of the value of the culture.

Accountability

We are good at the disciplines that result in high performance.

Some firms have developed accountability habits. Their people believe it is just not acceptable to miss targets. Performance accountability becomes a firm capability when employees realize that they must meet their performance expectations. Accountability comes when strategies translate into measurable standards of performance and when rewards are linked to these measurable standards of performance. When there is a line of sight between rewards, appraisals, and strategies, accountability is likely to follow. A leader who looks at an employee's performance appraisal form should know the strategy the employee is attempting to accomplish and what specific actions the employee should take to help accomplish the strategy. Rewards, both financial and non-financial, then reinforce the strategy and enable employees to receive clear, definitive, and tangible feedback on their performance.

Accountability can be monitored. When you look at a performance appraisal form, you should be able to see the strategy of the business. Are the items measured on the appraisal indicative of the strategy? What percentage of employees receive an appraisal each year? How much variance is there in compensation based on employee performance? Some firms say they have a pay-for-performance philosophy, but their annual increases all range from 3.5 to 4.5 percent. They claim an accountability culture, but they do not have one. What percentage of employees feel they have received a helpful feedback session in the past year? What percentage of employees feel that a portion of their compensation is at risk contingent on personal or team performance?

Collaboration

We are good at working across boundaries to ensure both efficiency and leverage.

The whole needs to be greater than the sum of the parts. Some organizations would be more valuable if their parts were operationally and legally independent than they are while they remain together. Such organizations frequently do not understand collaboration as a capability. Collaboration can come when the combined organization gains efficiencies of operation through sharing services, technology, sales efforts, or economies of scale. Collaboration can also come when the combined organization accomplishes more than its elements could accomplish separately because it has mastered learning and sharing ideas across boundaries; developing, allocating, and sustaining resources to key areas; and creating strategies that take full advantage of products and customers. Leaders build collaboration by seeking both efficiencies and synergistic feedback loops throughout the organization.

Collaboration can be tracked at both the institution and team levels. Institutionally, you can determine your breakup value and compare it with your current market value. In general, if the breakup value is 25 percent more than the current market value of the assets, collaboration is not occurring the way it should. Within the organization, collaboration can be tracked by monitoring the flow of talent and ideas across boundaries. Are people moving from one area to another? Are ideas or practices developed in one part of the firm being picked up in another part of the firm? Finally, collaboration can be measured by cost savings in administration through shared services. For example, shared services have been found to produce 15–25 percent cost savings in employee administrative costs. The average large firm spends about $1,600 per employee per year in administration, making it possible to calculate the probable cost savings of shared services: $1,600 × .2 [the cost savings] × number of employees.

Learning

We are good at generating and generalizing ideas with impact.

Learning consists of two separate but equally important steps: generating new ideas and generalizing (sharing) them across the organization. Generating new ideas comes from benchmarking (seeing what others have done and adapting it), experimentation (trying new things to see if and how they work), competence acquisition (hiring or developing people with new skills and ideas), and continuous improvement (building on what was done through suggestion systems and process analysis). Generalizing ideas means that the ideas move across a boundary of time (from one leader to the next), level (from one organizational layer to another), space (from one place to another), or division (from one business unit to another). Sharing ideas across boundaries can be done through technology, creating communities of practice, or moving people. Leaders who encourage individual and team learning can also create organizational learning through these practices.

Like collaboration, learning can be tracked at individual or organizational levels. For individuals, learning means letting go of old practices and adopting or adapting new ones. You can ask employees questions like these: What is the half-life of knowledge in your current job? When is 50 percent of what you know how to do out of date? What percentage of your personal value to the company comes from ideas that you have generated in the last year? How many people throughout the company are using ideas that you have generated? Such questions explore the extent to which employees are focused on generating and generalizing new ideas for their work. Learning within the organization shows up in continuous improvement. Are they getting better at production? Marketing? Customer service? Employee engagement? By establishing baselines and tracking results, you can make learning a part of the organizational improvement effort.

Leadership

We are good at embedding leaders throughout the organization who deliver the right results in the right way—who carry our leadership brand.

Some organizations produce leaders. These organizations generally have a leadership brand, or clear statement, of what leaders should know, be, and do. A leadership brand exists when the leaders from top to bottom of an organization have a unique identity connected to customer expectations. These leaders are recognizable, focused, and able to turn customer expectations into employee actions. In *Leadership Brand*, we discuss a six-step process for building such a brand in some detail.

The leadership brand can be tracked by monitoring the pool of future leaders. How many backups do we have in place for our top 100 employees? In one company, this figure dropped from about 3:1 (three qualified backups for each of the top hundred positions) to about .7:1 (less than one to one). This company recognized that its downsizing had seriously impaired its leadership bench strength.

Customer Connection

We are good at building enduring relationships of trust with targeted customers.

Many firms have discovered through customer value analysis that 20 percent of customers account for 80 percent of business performance. These customers become absolutely critical for a firm to compete and win. Customer connectivity can originate in a variety of practices: databases that identify and track individual customer preferences, dedicated account teams that build long-term relationships with targeted accounts, or involving a customer in the firm's HR practices. To build on such opportunities, many firms are including customers in staffing, training, compensation, and communication practices. Customer connectivity can also be enhanced when large proportions of the employee population have meaningful exposure to or interaction with external customers. The net result of these activities is to connect the hearts and minds of key customers to the hearts and minds of employees. When this happens, increased sales and market share are natural by-products.

Customer connectivity and service can be tracked through share of targeted customers rather than market share. This requires that you identify your key accounts, then track the share of those key accounts over time. In addition, regular customer service scores can offer insight on how well targeted customers recognize and regard your connectivity.

Innovation

We are good at doing something new in both content and process.

Innovation focuses on share of opportunity by creating the future rather than relying on past successes. Innovation matters because it fosters growth. It excites employees by focusing on what can be, anticipates customer requests and delights customers with what they did not expect, and builds confidence with investors by creating intangible value.

Business and HR leaders who focus on innovation constantly ask, What's next? They ask this in all domains of their business. Innovative product offerings include revolutionary new products or product extensions (that is, added features, performance, or functionality). Business strategy innovation changes how the enterprise makes money (new products or services), where the enterprise does business (opening up new regions of the world), how the enterprise goes to market (via new channels), how customers experience the firm (its brand identity), or how the firm serves customers (as when eBay discovered it could grow by helping customers sell things to each other). Administrative innovation occurs when new processes are introduced in finance, IT, marketing, HR, manufacturing, or other staff systems.

Innovation can be tracked through a vitality index such as the percent of revenues (or profits) that originate from products or services created in the last three years. Innovation can also be monitored through the introduction and deployment of new processes in the organization.

Strategic Unity

We are good at articulating and sharing a strategic point of view.

Many leaders tend to be better at formulating strategies than at accomplishing them. Often this comes because there is not a unity of shared understanding of the desired strategy. Four agendas (intellectual, behavioral, process, measurement) go into creating strategic unity. An *intellectual agenda* assures that employees from top to bottom share both what the strategy is and why it is important. This agenda is delivered through simple messages repeated constantly. A *behavioral agenda* assures that the ideas in the strategy shape how employees behave. This comes less by telling employees what to do and more by asking employees what they will do given the strategy. By allowing employees to define their behaviors relative to strategy, you make it possible for them to become committed to it. A *process agenda* ensures that the organization's processes (budgeting, hiring, decision making) align with strategy. These processes can be reengineered to ensure that they create unity. A *measurement agenda* ensures that all employees have a shared operational definition of the strategy and a means of measuring progress toward the accomplishment of the strategy. When all four agendas are in place, strategic unity is likely to follow.

Tracking strategic unity comes when employees have strategic literacy as evidenced by a common answer to the question, What is the strategy of this business that sets us apart from competitors and helps us win with customers? The behavioral agenda for strategic unity is measured by asking employees what percentage of the time they feel they are doing work that facilitates the strategy and by asking them if their suggestions for improvement are heard and acted on. The process agenda for strategic unity is measured by the extent to which processes logically and empirically link directly to the business strategy. The measurement agenda for strategic unity can be measured by the extent to which strategic goals and their accompanying measurements are shared throughout the company.

Simplicity

We are good at keeping strategies, processes, and products simple.

The quality, Six Sigma, and lean manufacturing movements have helped organizations reduce variance and reengineer processes. We see a number of firms today building on this work as they try to simplify how they work. This simplification can occur in how customers buy (from purchasing to delivery to payment), in how products are designed (for ease of use), and in how administrative processes function (such as processing benefits or attending a training program).

Simplicity can be measured by time per unit of activity (see Speed on page 39), by cost per unit, by reduction of redundant or unnecessary steps in work activities, and by moderating SKUs and complexity. One company found that each additional product option in its catalog cost $10,000, mostly hidden in design resources, inventory, and manufacturing costs.

Social Responsibility

We are good at contributing to the communities in which we operate or to the broader good.

In Europe, many firms now rely on what they call the "triple bottom line," where they measure the extent to which they meet high social responsibility standards. In addition, an increasing number and variety of mutual funds emphasize investments in companies that demonstrate social responsibility. Social responsibility shows up in various ways. Corporate giving, or philanthropy, represents a commitment to serving the community in which you operate. One company wanted to be known as a "corporation with a giving heart" and committed to donate to worthy community causes. Sustainability, or reducing the carbon footprint, is another form of social responsibility. Many firms are managing facilities (lighting, energy use, space) and product features (reducing packaging and using green products) and auditing energy consumption. Worker-friendly practices like family leave and flexible work arrangements help companies demonstrate their social responsibility. Being sensitive to the needs of local populations whose land contains substantial resources is an increasingly important aspect of corporate social responsibility. All of these socially responsible activities are woven around shared beliefs, values, and commitment to the community in which you operate.

Social responsibility can be tracked by both activity and reputation. Activity means that you have designed and implemented sustainability, philanthropy, and employability policies that communicate your social responsibility values. For example, some firms commit a portion of earnings to charity and also report the amount of employee time donated each year to serving others. Social reputation can be measured by indexes like Best Managed Companies where external bodies assess a firm's reputation.

Risk

We are good at anticipating and managing risk.

In economically uncertain times, organizations face changes that they cannot anticipate. Managing risk means having less disruption when things go wrong. When organizational resources are stretched to their limit, companies are less able to manage disruption. These resources may be financial or emotional. With tightly stretched capital, organizations cannot survive downturns or invest in new opportunities. In a similar vein, emotional resources can also be thinly stretched; employees can have too few emotional reserves to cope with additional change and face burnout. Managing risk increases an organization's ability to predict the future from the present. Reducing variance also helps reduce risk by building predictability and discipline into the processes of work.

Risk can be tracked by assessing the extent to which an organization's demands have exceeded its resources in financial markets and human needs. Is your organization overdrawn by having excessive debt or credit? Has your organization overtapped the emotional reserve of your employees? This can show up in mental health care costs, turnover, lower productivity, or lower attitude scores. The capacity to manage risk well can be essential to strategy implementation, especially in a volatile economy.

Efficiency

We are good at managing costs of operation.

In competitive markets, managing costs efficiently increases the freedom that a firm has to invest in high-return activities. Leaders can reduce costs through processes, people, and projects. Process improvements come through Kaizen or other productivity improvement efforts that reduce variance, remove steps in getting work done, reduce inventories and work space, and ensure a flow of products and services. People improvements come from doing more with less through technology, teams, and more efficient processes. Project investments come from managing capital spending to allocate money wisely for future investments. Leaders who only manage costs and ignore growth fail because you cannot save your way to prosperity; leaders who avoid cost and efficiency improvements are unlikely to have the opportunity to grow the top line.

Tracking efficiency can be the easiest of all. Costs of goods sold, inventories, direct and indirect labor, and capital employed can all be measured from the balance sheet and income statement.

Conclusion

The capabilities in this chapter represent the outcomes of the HR transformation. They are the deliverables of human resources, and they lead to the outcomes for each stakeholder (as shown in Figure 3.1). In focusing on capabilities as outcomes, the HR transformation team should do a capability audit where they identify which capabilities are most critical to their organization's future success given business conditions and business strategy. With those prioritized capabilities, scorecards can be created to track baseline and progress in the critical capabilities. By focusing on both stakeholder and organizational capability outcomes, the result of the HR transformation can be defined and tracked.

Figure 3.1 Diagram of Stakeholder Measures

TOOL 3.3	*Operationalizing Your Capabilities*
	Turn the capabilities identified in the capability audit into specific measures that can be monitored and tracked. Watch a video of Mark Nyman describing how to connect the deliverables of the transformation in a scorecard such that everyone knows the desired results and how well the organization is meeting those results.
	▶ *Go to www.TransformHR.com*

TOOL 3.4	*Mapping Capabilities to Stakeholders*
	Listen to Justin Allen share best-practice examples of how to show that the development of your key capabilities will benefit employees, line managers, customers, investors, communities, and other stakeholders.
	▶ *Go to www.TransformHR.com*

Phase 3:

HR REDESIGN

CHAPTER 4

REDESIGN THE HR DEPARTMENT

4

The first two phases of HR transformation answer the questions *why* (business context) and *what* (outcomes of HR transformation). The third phase addresses *how* to do the transformation. This phase has three components, each of which is a way of defining what we mean by HR:

- The HR function or department may need to be redesigned.
- HR practices may be transformed to be more effectively or more fully aligned, integrated, and innovative.
- HR professionals may be upgraded to possess the competencies required to do their work.

In this chapter, we begin our answer to the how question by focusing on the makeover of the HR department, because it is the beginning of many HR transformation efforts. The essence of a transformed HR department is the orientation to run the HR department like a business within a business. Any business has both a strategy (what it is trying to do) and a structure (how it organizes people and work to get things done). Both HR strategy and structure can be redesigned to make sure that the HR department responds to business context and delivers value to the organization.

Transformation of the HR Strategy

An HR strategy gives focus and direction to the HR department. There are many versions and dimensions of strategy statements in general and HR in particular. We suggest that in transforming the strategy of a specific HR department, the statement of strategy (sometimes called strategic direction, intent, or architecture) should answer three questions, in this order:

1. Who are you? (vision)
2. What do you deliver? (mission or value proposition)
3. Why do you do it? (the results we want to achieve)

Who You Are

Who you are represents an identity or image, which is what an HR strategy should offer those outside as well as inside the function. This identity shapes both stakeholder and internal HR professional expectations, focuses on the future rather than the past, aligns with business requirements, and offers a stretch goal. It shapes the brand of the HR function, creates expectations, gives direction, and guides development.

You might describe the identity through the roles and actions performed by HR professionals including facilitators, coaches, architects, partners, planners, contributors, thought leaders, creators, players, or executors. You will likely build your identity with more than one of these descriptors, but you should have enough strategic focus to select no more than three. This identity should be tested and confirmed with line managers who use your services, with employees who are affected by policies you create, with customers and investors whose relationship with your firm is shaped by your policies, and within the HR function by your HR professionals. For example, in this context, the identity might be given as "thought leaders and change architects" or "facilitators and coaches."

This identity is often drafted by the senior HR team with input from key stakeholders who want to help craft a statement of what they want the function to be known for. Thus, the identity has a reality component as well as an aspirational component. We have found a simple question helps frame the definition of identity: What are the top three things you (in HR) want to be known for by those who use your services?

What You Deliver

What you deliver is the set of outcomes described in Chapter 3. These outcomes should include the capabilities an organization needs to succeed, which can also be characterized as the intangibles an organization promises its investors. For example, an HR department might ensure productivity, build individual talent, increase speed, establish a shared mind-set, improve accountability, or foster innovation. These capabilities that help deliver a strategy become the deliverables of HR. In an HR strategy, these outcomes should be operationalized so that they can be tracked and measured. Both HR professionals and line managers are accountable for their delivery. Defining HR deliverables comes from doing organizational audits as described in Chapter 3.

Why You Do It

This question links to business context (Chapter 2) and specific business results tied to key stakeholders. This part of the HR strategy builds on the "so that" statement and can include increased revenue, customer share, customer loyalty, or total market return. These "so that" statements should imply measures that allow you to monitor the progress human resources makes and the impact it has on the business. Again, you will likely select more than one result (that is, more than one organizational capability to focus on) but should have enough focus to select no more than three. There will probably be things that people in HR are working to achieve that don't fit into these primary descriptors, but the descriptors should reflect the strategic work of HR in your organization. With these measurable outcomes, HR has a clear direction.

Putting the three statements together creates your HR Strategy Statement:

Part A: Who we are:

We are _____, _____, and _____

Part B: What we do:

who _____, _____, and _____

Part C: Why we do it

so that _____, _____, and _____.

While this formulaic statement should be adapted to your circumstances, it should represent a clear definition of your HR strategy that can then be communicated both inside and outside the HR function.

TOOL 4.1	*HR Strategy Statement*
	Download a copy of the HR Strategy Statement Worksheet and use this document as a template in your HR strategy clarification meeting.
	▶ *Go to www.TransformHR.com*

TOOL 4.2	*Drafting a Powerful HR Strategy*
	Learn from Wayne Brockbank as he describes how to draft an HR strategy and then how to make it real.
	▶ *Go to www.TransformHR.com*

Transformation of the HR Organization

Transforming an HR department requires building an HR organization that reflects both the business organization and the HR strategy. We have found three overriding organizational design principles: first, make the HR organization follow the logic and structure of the business organization. Second, make the HR organization follow the flow of any professional service organization. Third, differentiate between transactional and transformational HR work.

The HR organization adds value when its logic and structure reflect the logic and structure of the company that it serves. We have found that companies often organize their businesses along two dimensions: centralized (to drive efficiency and control) and decentralized (to drive effectiveness and flexibility). A company whose portfolio strategy is based on a holding company configuration consists of multiple business units who are independent of each other (bottom right of Figure 4.1). Competitive business decisions are made in the local operating divisions. In such cases, HR logic and processes are likewise to be found in the business units. In most holding companies, corporate HR is relatively small or nonexistent. At the other extreme is a corporation that consists of a single business (top left). In this case, the corporation and the business unit are the same. Thus corporate HR and business unit HR are likewise the same.

The relatively more complicated portfolio configurations are alternative levels of diversification that range from unrelated to highly related (top right of Figure 4.1). In a corporation whose business portfolio logic is based on unrelated diversification, the differences across the business strongly outweigh

Figure 4.1 Types of Organizational Design

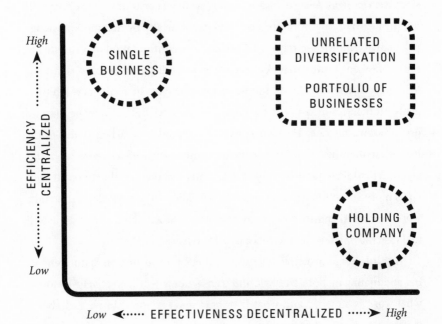

the similarities. In these conditions, the HR logic will tend to be established and customized to the differing local businesses. The HR danger in companies with unrelated diversification is the "one size fits all" trap. Care must be taken to ensure that HR strategies and practices are customized to fit the logic of business requirements.

Under corporate portfolios that are configured on the assumptions of related diversification, the similarities across the businesses strongly outweigh the differences. In this case, HR logic, strategies, and practices will be shared across the business units. The HR dangers in this configuration are redundancies in design and delivery of HR practices and the suboptimization of business synergy. The rule of thumb to be followed is that the HR strategy and structure should mirror those of the company. Some have argued that our recommended HR structure fails in small companies. They do not understand that centralized (and often small) business should have centralized HR structures.

The second organizational design principle for HR is that of any professional service firm. A law firm, advertising agency, accounting firm, or consulting firm earns recognition, respect, and client loyalty by making knowledge productive. Knowledge represents the collective information and insights of the profession. Productivity occurs when these insights become standards for how to work with clients and when these insights help clients reach their goals. Human resources rests on a body of knowledge about how people and organizations operate. These insights become productive when clients of the HR department use that knowledge to improve their effectiveness and efficiency. The stakeholders described in Chapter 2 should be able to reach their goals more smoothly because of the organization of the HR department, its work processes, and its day-to-day operations. Strategic HR work done well makes achieving business results easier for business leaders.

A third design principle for successful HR transformation is differentiating and managing both strategic and transactional work effectively. Defining what work is strategic and what is transactional is not a simple task, but it is paramount in transformation. We suggested in Chapter 1 that a common mistake of HR transformation is to make administrative HR changes without addressing more strategic issues. The work described in Chapter 2 and Chapter 3 about business context and key capabilities creates the context for knowing what HR work in your business is or should be strategic. Once this is done, the process involves evaluating each and every HR output and determining how the output contributes to the business. It also requires making sure that the administrative or transactional work is done efficiently.

Unless strategic work and transactional work are separated, neither gets done well. Until you can specifically identify which HR work has the most business impact, you don't have the clarity and focus required to be a strategic partner. This process enables you to make your HR strategy real. Also, HR organizations that don't do transactional work flawlessly are not credible when they attempt to play strategic roles. Again, making sure that strategic work and transactional work are not marbled together will make both kinds of work more effective.

TOOL 4.3	*Strategic vs. Transactional Work*
▶	As seen in the Pfizer case (see Chapter 10) separating transactional from transformational work is an essential step in any HR transformation. Listen to Mark Nyman describe the sifting process.
	▶ *Go to www.TransformHR.com*

Building on these three design principles, the evolving HR organization can have five distinct and at times overlapping sets of responsibilities. These five responsibilities represent channels or ways of doing HR work, as outlined in Figure 4.2. The HR department might choose to create a specific organizational structure or division for each channel, or it might not. The critical issue is to identify the flow of work for each of the five channels in the HR organization and to upgrade each channel to deliver the outcomes discussed in Chapter 3. Additionally, awareness of all five channels is helpful in identifying both current and future HR outputs to ensure all outputs are included in your analysis. At times, some try to transform the HR department by focusing on one channel. For example, putting in a new HR information system (Channel 1 in the figure) can increase the efficiency of doing HR administrative work, but this is not a complete HR transformation unless the other roles are also redesigned (as specified in the third design principle).

Figure 4.2 Overview of the HR Organization

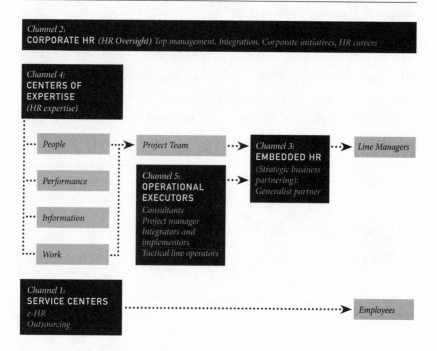

HR Channel 1: Service Centers

Service centers emerged in the late 1990s as HR leaders (and leaders of other functional organizations such as IT, finance, and purchasing) realized that many administrative tasks are more efficiently performed in a centralized, standardized way. The maturation of information technology has also contributed to the growth of service centers and their transfer to lower-cost parts of the world (such as India or Eastern Europe). As one HR executive said, "If we move the HR work 400 yards, we might as well move it 3,000 miles."

Service centers enjoy economies of scale for traditional HR work such as employee assistance programs, relocation administration, benefits claims processing, pension plan enrollment and administration, applicant tracking, payroll, and learning administration. Service centers require a standardization of HR processes, thus reducing redundancy and duplication, and they can also be accessible 24 hours a day, 7 days a week, from inside or outside the company because of technology. Transformation of service centers comes primarily through technology-enabled employee self-service, outsourcing, or both.

Technology-Enabled Employee Self-Service Centers

Properly designed technology enables employees to manage much of their own HR administrative work. The popular term emerging for this trend is *self-service*. Employees can also take care of many routine transactions whenever they wish, because automated systems don't keep office hours. We estimate that employees themselves can answer 60 percent of their HR questions or transactions—finding 401(k) investment choices, for example—online. In transforming technology-based solutions, HR professionals need to be aware of the following choices:

Customization and Building from Scratch or Buying off the Shelf

Companies often regard themselves as unique, but in today's world, it is best to avoid designing and implementing a unique HR data portal and service or to significantly customize one. One company spent thousands of hours creating its unique HRIT system only to wind up with something that simply wasn't as good as what it could have been bought off the shelf for a fraction of the cost. Many effective HRIT products are on the market, and adapting one of them is much easier and less expensive than building something new or massively customizing a purchased system.

Emphasizing Efficiency or Close Employee Relationships

The employee's goal for many HR transactions is to finish as quickly and easily as possible. Nonetheless, HR is not like retail banking, where customers happily manage transactions by ATM and do not want a personal relationship with the bank. It is more like investment banking, where relationships still offer the best long-term approach to customer share. Relationship HR, designed to build loyalty between individual employees and the firm, likewise offers the best long-term approach to employee care. Much—if not most—of this will come through the effective implementation of the strategic HR work. However, it is important to build into the HRIT system the option for employees to get help from real people when needed.

Gathering Data or Generating Information

One clear benefit of self-service is the ability to collect data on trends and needs. For example, knowing how many younger and older employees use e-learning can help in planning and employee communication. But data does not improve decision making unless it is used. Data that is warehoused in files and never fully deployed might as well not exist. Good business decisions start with good questions that require managerial insight and foresight; then, data collected through technology-based self-service can be used to assess alternatives and test hypotheses.

Collecting Data or Maintaining Privacy

Concerns over privacy continue to be a major challenge. The more data accumulates, the more the firm knows about the employee, and the harder it is to keep the data secure. As useful and convenient as 24/7 access to employee data can be, it blurs the boundaries between work and social life. While each employee needs to find ways to manage this balance, technology can become increasingly intrusive and inhibit the work-life balance that helps give employees purpose and meaning at work and at home.

Archiving or Updating Information

Too often in building an HR information system, the focus is on the creation of the system, not its maintenance. Just as new buildings need 15–20 percent of the total cost budgeted for annual maintenance, HRIT investments should factor in an additional 15–20 percent of the original costs as a budget for annual operations. This means updating information on the system as well as periodic updates of the system itself.

Outsourced Service Centers

Outsourcing draws on the premise that knowledge and process capacity are assets that can be tapped without ownership. HR expertise can be shared across boundaries by alliances in which two or more firms together create a common service or by outright purchase from vendors who specialize in offering it. In transforming HR through outsourcing, the vendors take advantage of economies of knowledge and scale. Economies of knowledge allow them to keep up with the latest HR research and technology. Economies of process scale make it possible to invest in facilities and technologies beyond what is realistic for a single company. Firms like Hewitt, Accenture, and Towers Perrin are therefore able to offer bundles of HR services with the goal of moving client companies away from the traditional idea of outsourcing to multiple vendors—one for staffing, another for training, another for compensation, and so on—all taking somewhat different approaches to their work.

Companies using HR outsourcing increasingly seek integrated solutions rather than isolated practices. Though outsourcing on this scale is too new for results to be definitive, these firms have experienced several potential benefits:

Cost Savings

Savings have been in the 20–25 percent range—a substantial amount for large companies, which spend an average of $1,600 per employee per year on administration. Firms with ten thousand employees, for example, could estimate saving $3.2 million per year (20 percent of $1,600 per employee × 10,000 employees).

Standardization and Simplicity

Outsourcing requires consistent HR transactions. Many large firms have grown through mergers and acquisitions, accumulating diverse HR systems. Simply contracting out this work forces a level of consistency that might take years to accomplish internally.

Increased Speed and Quality of Service

As we mentioned, outsourcing vendors generally rely on technology and have the economies of scale to stay up to date with new developments that continuously improve their services. Employees often perceive service as actually improving with effective outsourcing.

HR Focus

Outsourcing transactional HR work enables HR professionals to focus on more strategic work. Thus, outsourcing increases the likelihood that HR professionals will become more strategic in thought and action.

As you transform, these benefits need to be analyzed over a longer time to confirm the value of outsourcing. Nonetheless, while early indicators suggest that outsourcing offers positive returns, it has risks and pitfalls as well. Some organizations have been very pleased with outsourcing parts of HR and others have had a very bad experience with the same parts. We have found some common challenges for outsourcing: picking the wrong vendor, not managing contracts well, underinvesting in the change management required to implement HR outsourcing, governing the different roles within the new HR organization, and coping with loss of formal control. Despite these risks, we believe large firms will continue to outsource bundles of HR transactions to increasingly viable vendors. Smaller firms will probably outsource individual HR practices such as payroll and benefits administration. Both types of outsourcing reflect the collaborative work across boundaries that will character-ize the organizations of the future.

The transformation of HR through service centers requires cooperation of HR and IT professionals. HR can specify the content or practices that need to be more efficiently administered and IT can design the systems to make this happen.

HR Channel 2: Corporate HR (HR Oversight)

The corporate HR role can be redesigned to address six important responsibilities, which are discussed in the sections that follow:

- They create a consistent firmwide culture and identity.
- They shape the programs that implement the CEO's agenda.
- They design processes to make sure that HR work aligns to business goals.
- They arbitrate disputes between centers of expertise and embedded HR.
- They take primary responsibility for HR services of corporate-level employees.
- They ensure HR professional development.

First, the work of corporate HR professionals creates a consistent cultural identity for the corporation. No matter how diversified the business strategy, unless the company is truly a holding company that operates as an investment portfolio, a variety of important external stakeholders form relationships with the entire firm. Shareholders tend to care mainly about overall performance, and large customers who do considerable business with the firm tend to engage with multiple divisions. Likewise, the image of the entire firm is gen-erally what attracts potential employees to specific divisions. Corporate HR professionals build or reinforce the firm's culture and reputation by focusing on values and principles. Line managers own the principles, but corporate HR is the group in charge of institutionalizing these principles.

Second, corporate HR professionals shape the programs that implement the CEO's agenda. Most CEOs have a corporate strategic agenda, such as globalization, product innovation, customer service, or social responsibility. Corporate HR professionals are expected to convert this agenda into a plan for investment and action and to build organizational readiness to deliver this agenda by defining capabilities, designing HR practices, and facilitating action plans to deliver corporation-wide HR work. Corporate HR ensures that shared business requirements result in shared HR principles and practices.

Third, corporate HR is responsible for making sure that HR work done within the corporation is aligned to business goals. Corporate HR can create and mandate a clear process for linking business strategy and HR that can be adapted to each unit. Corporate HR referees debates on sameness versus difference in HR practices across operations and specific businesses. This is much more easily done when there is clarity on what HR work is transformational and what work is transactional. In addition, corporate HR should ensure that business unit HR is involved in setting measurable objectives. In highly diversified firms, corporate HR will probably not dictate what the measurable objectives will be, but it should shoulder responsibility for ensuring that HR goals are set and results are measured.

Fourth, corporate HR professionals arbitrate disputes between centers of expertise and embedded HR (HR professionals within the businesses or operations). Centers of expertise naturally lean toward consistency, while embedded HR professionals prefer flexibility and choice in response to the (seemingly) unique needs of their stakeholders. Corporate HR will not have a magic answer or uniform formula for deciding when to standardize practices and when to vary them, but it can create forums for discussion of the trade-offs and choices and work through disagreements to reach a win-win or good compromise. We call this managing the push (centers of expertise) and pull (embedded HR) that requires conversation and, at times, arbitration.

Fifth, corporate HR professionals take primary responsibility for nurturing corporate-level employees—a role both like and unlike that of HR elsewhere in the firm. Like all employees, corporate employees should perform their transaction HR work through service centers or technology. However, some corporate employees are unique in that their relationship with the firm is visible and symbolic. Public reports of executive compensation, for example, require extra care to ensure the right messages are communicated to all internal and external stakeholders. Senior HR professionals also frequently play significant roles in coaching senior executives, offering advice ranging from personal leadership style to dealing with key employee transitions and succession issues to observations and assistance in evolving the corporate culture.

Finally, corporate HR is responsible for ensuring ongoing HR professional development. Too often, HR professionals are the cobbler's barefoot children—designing learning experiences and developmental opportunities for others, for example, while going without a similar investment in their own growth and development. HR corporate staff should pay attention to the growth needs of HR professionals, particularly those associated with HR transformation. Changing the impact of HR requires HR professionals to unlearn old roles and ways of working and to learn new ones.

As the corporate HR channel is redesigned, these six responsibilities should be taken into account so that corporate HR professionals have clear expectations.

HR Channel 3: Embedded HR (Strategic Business Partnering)

In shared service organizations, some HR professionals work in organizational units defined by geographic location, product line, or functions such as R&D or engineering. These HR professionals, whom we call "embedded HR," go by many titles: relationship managers, HR business partners, or HR generalists. Whatever their specific title, they work directly with line managers and each organizational unit leadership team to clarify strategy, perform organizational audits, manage talent and organization, create value-adding organizational capabilities, deliver supportive HR strategies, and lead their HR function. In redesigning embedded HR professionals' roles, a number of their responsibilities should be clarified:

- They engage in and support business strategy assessment and review.
- They represent employee interests and are attentive to implications of change.
- They define requirements to reach business goals and identify where problems may exist.
- They select and implement the HR practices that are most appropriate for the delivery of the business strategy.
- They measure and track performance to see whether the HR investments made by the business deliver the intended value.

In the first role, embedded HR professionals engage in and support business strategy, offering insights and helping leaders to identify where their organization can and should invest resources to win new business ventures or increase existing investments' performance. They help to frame the process of business strategy development, are proactive in providing insights into business issues, have a personal vision of the future of the business, and facilitate effective strategy development discussions within the management team. As we discuss in *HR Competencies*, the results of the most recent survey show that this role reflects a competency we have elsewhere called the "strategic architect."

In the course of supporting strategic decision making, HR professionals also represent employee interests by highlighting the implications of strategic choices. For example, how much of the workforce needs to be retrained, reorganized, or resized? HR professionals help develop a clear strategic message that can be communicated to employees and translated into action. In the process, they watch out for the tendency to groupthink, encouraging everyone to participate and clearly valuing dissent while seeking consensus.

Throughout the strategy formulation and implementation process, embedded HR professionals audit the organization to define what is required to reach the goals and where problems may exist. Sometimes this is an informal process whereby HR professionals reflect on and raise concerns about strategy delivery capabilities. As we discuss in "Capitalizing on Capabilities," other audits can involve a formal 360-degree review to determine what capabilities are required and available given the strategy (see Chapter 3). These audits will help assess consistency between the internal corporate culture and the culture required to make customers and investors happy on the outside. In doing these organizational audits, embedded HR professionals partner with line managers and collect data that lead to focused action.

Based on organizational audit information, embedded HR professionals select and implement the HR practices most appropriate for delivering the business strategy. In doing so, they are expected to bring their unique knowledge of the business and its people in selecting practices that add value, integrating them to deliver capabilities, and sequencing them to ensure implementation. Embedded HR professionals pull guidance and support from HR specialists who reside in centers of expertise and adapt this input to the requirements of the business. This process of accessing rather than owning resources means that embedded HR professionals must be adept at influencing and working collaboratively with colleagues. They must be able to negotiate with their HR counterparts in centers of expertise who have mandated corporate agendas. They must be effective at managing multiple temporary teams.

Finally, embedded HR professionals measure and track performance to see whether the HR investments made by the business deliver their intended value. In essence, embedded HR professionals diagnose what needs to be done, broker resources to get these things done, and monitor progress to make sure they have gotten done.

In redesigning the embedded HR channel, these responsibilities should be delineated and understood so that embedded HR professionals know what is expected of them.

HR Channel 4: Centers of Expertise (HR Expertise)

Centers of expertise operate as specialized consulting firms inside the organization. Depending on the size of the enterprise, they may be corporation-wide or regional or country-based. They often act like businesses that have multiple clients (business units) using their services. In some cases, a fee for use or a "chargeback" formula plus an overhead charge for basic services may fund them. Centers are demand-pull operations—if businesses do not value their services, they will not continue. Center-of-expertise HR professionals play a number of important roles that should be clarified in an HR transformation:

- They create service menus aligned with the capabilities driving business strategy.
- They diagnose needs and recommend services most appropriate to the situation.
- They collaborate with embedded HR professionals in selecting and implementing the right services.
- They create new menu offerings if the current offerings are insufficient.
- They manage the menu.
- They shepherd the learning community within the organization.

As internal design and process consultants, HR professionals in centers of expertise create menus of HR best practices. The menus lay out choices of what has been or could be done to deliver high-quality human resources. Embedded HR professionals are expected to choose from these menus, which legitimizes the HR practices in use company-wide. HR professionals in centers will constantly be updating and tweaking the menus based on latest best-practice research and experience within the company.

In a similar vein, a second role of the center-of-expertise HR professional is to work with embedded HR professionals to select the right practice or intervention for specific situations. For example, say an embedded HR generalist realizes the need for a first-line supervisory training program. The center of expertise should already have a menu of choices available to individual organizations. For example, the menu of choices might consist of an in-house workshop, some externally provided workshops (through consultants or a local university), a self-directed DVD program, self-paced computer learning exercises, a 360-degree feedback exercise, and other development experiences. If a current menu doesn't exist, the design experts will assemble one based on their knowledge of the field and the company. A process expert takes this menu to the embedded HR professional and helps diagnose the need and select the services most appropriate for the business and situation, offering advice on how to implement the selected choices. The embedded HR professional is responsible for making the selection and for implementing the right development experiences for improving first-line supervision.

As a third important role, the center is expected to collaborate with the embedded professional in making the selection and in supporting the implementation. If the embedded HR professionals and center-of-expertise HR professionals agree that existing menu items are not sufficient, the design experts create new solutions that will then be added to the menu for the enterprise.

That is the fourth role: the creation of new offerings when the current slate is insufficient or inadequate for the need. In many cases, the need for additional menu offerings will be prompted by a company acquisition or decision to diversify and invest in new businesses. For example, we earlier mentioned the growth of IBM into global consulting services. As the organization shifted from products to services, new HR offerings were established to respond to the changing needs.

This points out the next role of the center of expertise—to manage the size and breadth of the process or service menu. In general, menu size will depend on the degree of business diversification. In related diversification, the menus will be smaller, ensuring that different businesses use similar management practices; in unrelated diversification, the menus will be larger, allowing more flexibility and choice. In all cases, the center of expertise needs to manage the boundaries of what is helpful, acceptable, and permitted. As a very simple example, a large regional bank conducted an audit of its training practices and discovered that twelve distinct coaching programs were used in various parts of the organization. The center of expertise reduced that number from twelve to one, with both a cost benefit to the organization (better contracting) and the creation of a common language and skill base in coaching.

Finally, centers of expertise also shepherd the learning community within the enterprise. They initiate learning when design experts generate new ideas for the menu, after which process experts generalize learning by sharing experiences across units. For example, they share the experiences of supervisory training from one unit to another so that each business does not have to create its own training programs. The process experts may transfer the learning, or they may have the requesting organizational unit communicate directly with those who have previously done the work.

An HR redesign should ensure that the accountabilities or centers are understood and accepted and that HR professionals in these roles have the abilities to meet these expectations. Those in the center have to stay current with HR processes and frameworks that can add value to the business, while not falling victim to the oft-repeated mistake of creating solutions looking for problems. The relationship between those in the center and those who are embedded in the business is a critical link to ensure this does not occur.

HR Channel 5: Operational Execution

A large number of HR departments have attempted to operationalize the model we've described, but many of them find that some work continues to fall through the cracks. While embedded HR professionals are asked and expected to be strategic and do organizational diagnosis, they often find themselves overwhelmed by operational HR work that conflicts with their main purpose and renders them unable to make high-value-added strategic contributions. They report that they spend a growing amount of time doing individual casework (for example, handling disciplinary issues), performing operational tasks (such as setting up and attending recruiting interviews), doing analysis and reporting (such as managing compensation reviews), or delivering initiatives (such as new employee orientation).

Service centers typically do not perform these operational tasks since they require personal attention; centers of expertise do not perform them since they usually require deep and unique knowledge of the business and strong internal business relationships; line managers do not perform them since they lack the technical expertise. Hence, embedded HR professionals feel drawn into this operational work by its sheer volume, even when they have the skills and self-confidence to be more strategic and are encouraged to focus on their transformational role.

What has been missing in some HR restructurings is the capacity to deliver and implement the operational tactics while maintaining focus on key business and customer issues. While this operational work ideally occurs through an integrated team, someone needs to be charged with responsibility for this team and how it works. We are finding that companies are responding to these missing implementation requirements in different ways:

- One company has established the role of "junior business partners" assigned to the HR generalists or business partners. These individuals are required to turn the strategic ideas into operational practice within the business.
- Another company created a team of HR operational consultants who are assigned to a business to help turn HR strategy into action. They focus on project work with an emphasis on implementing specific projects within the business. The consulting pool consists of HR professionals who are adept at making HR initiatives happen. The consulting pool secondarily serves as a preparatory and testing ground for individuals who are potential incumbents for senior embedded HR professional roles.
- Another company uses a case adviser who comes from the service center to follow through on employee requests.

All of these companies, and many others, are experimenting with how to solve this common problem: *how to make sure that HR implements state-of-the-art strategies tailored to the needs of the business.* We call this an operational exec-utor role. These HR professionals will be required to meld what the business requires for success (driven by the embedded HR professionals) with innova-tive and state-of-the-art HR practices (driven by the centers of expertise) into an operational plan that can be executed in a timely way.

Organizations thinking of creating an operational HR capability face some challenges that need to be addressed if the effort is to be successful. Our discussions with HR leaders suggest the following factors are particularly important:

Selecting the Right Individuals

Operational HR roles require a particular set of competencies. These roles are best for people who are execution- and implementation-oriented rather than focused on strategic relationships (embedded HR) or new knowledge creation (centers of expertise). However, operational HR roles can also be excellent developmental opportunities for both embedded and center professionals. In fact, HR departments at firms such as United Technologies, Textron, and Kel-logg consider success in an operational HR role a necessary step in qualifying for a more strategic role. We think that, over time, HR organizations will find that operational HR functions best as a mix of long-timers (people who like to do this work) and rotational resources.

Developing the Skills Needed to Be Successful

Project and implementation management skills are crucial for operational HR professionals, but so are team skills. They must quickly understand what is expected. They must bring together the embedded, business, and center-of-expertise HR professionals in clarifying goals, roles, specific actions, and measures. They must make the changes happen. Some diagnostic skills are also important; the construction of a project plan must, for example, take situational (and often political) dynamics into account, along with other competing activities. People who work in operational HR should not be seen as simply pairs of hands to implement but rather as involved early in the development of solutions.

Managing Priorities and Workloads

Choosing what projects are appropriate for operational HR is an important task. HR doesn't have infinite resources, and it is all too easy for HR to use its scarce operational HR resources on lower-priority work that other HR professionals do not want to do. This is a mistake as it trivializes both the operational HR work and the people who do the operational HR work. As a result, such marginalized HR personnel will leave. It is also a mistake to employ operational HR resources in a way that precludes the involvement and commitment of line leaders and other employees.

Maintaining Business Focus

In all considerations, operational HR must maintain an unrelenting focus on a business logic that is consistent with the logic of the corporate business portfolio. Regardless of whether the corporation is a single business unit, diversified, or a holding company, HR should maintain its focus on making the corporate business logic successful.

Measuring Contribution

Because operational HR is project- and implementation-oriented, how performance is measured should also be project-based and implementation-based.

This operational execution channel will continue to become clearer as these HR professionals make sure that HR investments turn into capabilities that deliver on the vision and goals of human resources.

Conclusion: Redesigning the HR Department

In this chapter, we lay out a two-step approach to redesigning an HR department. First, it requires a clear statement of the HR strategy. This statement comes from answering three questions. (Who are we? What do we deliver? And why do we do it?) This statement becomes the basis for further transformation work. Second, redesigning an HR department means understanding what work is strategic and what work is transactional. This sets a baseline for clarifying five channels through which HR work is delivered. It then allows you to organize the channels in a way that delivers the most value to the business. When the responsibilities of each of these five channels are defined and acted on, the department redesign has moved forward.

CHAPTER 5

HOW TO DO TRANSFORMATION

5

HR transformation requires clarifying the strategy and structure of the HR department, then focusing on enhancing the work of human resources. In this chapter, we offer a road map for transforming HR practices based on two dimensions:

- *Content:* What is the work of HR?
- *Process:* How can HR work be improved or reengineered?

These two dimensions combine in Figure 5.1 to provide an overview of how to transform HR practices.

Figure 5.1 Road Map for Enhancing HR Practices

ENHANCING HR PRACTICES		PROCESS: Ways to improve or reengineer HR practices		
		ALIGN	INTEGRATE	INNOVATE
CONTENT: Categories of HR practices	PEOPLE			
	PERFORMANCE			
	COMMUNICATION			
	WORK			

In the rows, we have clustered the work of HR into four categories: people, performance, communication, and work. This typology synthesizes the complex and varied array of HR practices that represent the HR playbook for both today and tomorrow. If HR is to be a decision science, as John Boudreau and Peter Ramstad describe it, all these domains of HR practice need to be refined and research needs to be performed, organized, and aggregated. In the columns, we have identified three ways to reengineer HR practices: alignment, integration, and innovation. When combined, these two dimensions lay out a blueprint or road map for how to improve HR practices. HR transformation means upgrading all HR practices in aligned, integrated, and innovative ways. As we note in Chapter 1, HR transformation is limited when HR practices are narrowly defined (for example, only focusing on either talent or people) or when HR practices are aligned with strategy but not offered as an integrated whole.

The Work of HR: Four Domains of HR Practice

People talk about the work of human resources as activities, systems, processes, decisions, or initiatives. We have chosen to talk about the work of HR as a set of HR practices because a practice is something that is continually being learned (we practice piano or sports). A practice is also activity within a profession (the practice of law), and the concept of best practice defines an activity that delivers an outcome better than some other activity. Transforming HR could mean changing as many as 120 separate HR practices. In *The HR Value Proposition*, we have synthesized this vast array of HR work into four domains that represent the flows or processes central to organization success:

- *Flow of people:* What happens to the organization's key asset—its people— including how people move in, through, up, and out of the organization. Proper attention to people flow ensures the availability and development of the talent the organization needs to accomplish its strategy.

- *Flow of performance management:* What links people to work—the standards and measures, financial and nonfinancial rewards, and feedback that reflect stakeholder interests. Proper attention to this flow promotes accountability for performance by defining, noting, and rewarding it—and penalizing its absence.
- *Flow of information:* What information do people need to do their work and how do they get the requisite information. Information can flow up, down, or laterally. It can flow from the outside in or from the inside out. Proper attention to information flow ensures that people know what is happening and why and can apply themselves to what needs doing to create value.
- *Flow of work:* Who does work, how work is done, where work is done, and how work is supported through business and operating processes to combine individual efforts into organizational outputs. Proper attention to work flow provides the governance, accountability, and physical setting that ensure high-quality results.

Transformation of HR practices requires recognizing emerging trends in each category and the revision of HR practices to be consistent with those trends. It is tempting in the field of HR today to separate and isolate these four streams. For example, a company might invest in talent management (hiring, promoting, retaining people) without expending the time, effort, and resources necessary to ensure that people have both the internal and external information required for high levels of commitment and performance. HR transformation is incomplete unless alignment, integration, and innovation occur for all four categories of HR processes. In our workshops with HR leaders and professionals, we find that only the best companies identify the synergies they might capture by working more closely together. For example, in a recent conference at British Airways, functional experts from across the four domains found a number of ways that staffing (people), compensation and benefits (performance), and organizational development (work) could very fruitfully collaborate. Narrow definitions of HR work result in narrow scopes of HR transformation.

People Practices: Flow of People

People practices refers to the talent within the organization. Talent management is the systematic process of creating and sustaining individual competencies that will help the business deliver strategy. Simply stated, companies with better talent will be more successful. A multitude of programs and investments have been made to attract, retain, and upgrade talent. Yet sometimes after stipulating that talent matters, it is easy to get lost in the myriad promises, programs, and processes and lose sight of the basics. At the risk of gross oversimplification, we suggest that there is actually a deceptively simple formula for talent that can help to transform talent practices:

TALENT = COMPETENCE × COMMITMENT × CONTRIBUTION

Competence

Competence means that individuals have the knowledge, skills, and values required for today's jobs—and tomorrow's. One company clarified competence as *right skills, right place, right job*. Competence clearly matters because incompetence leads to poor decision making. But without commitment, competence is discounted. Highly competent employees who are not committed are smart—but don't work very hard. Transforming HR practices related to competence means following four steps:

1. *Articulate a theory or set a standard.* Developing competence begins by identifying the required competencies to deliver future work. Rather than focus on what has worked in the past by comparing low- and high-performing employees, more recent competence standards come from turning future customer expectations into present employee requirements. At any level in a company, an HR professional can facilitate a discussion about these questions:
   • What are the *current* social and technical competencies we have within our company?

- What are the environmental changes facing our business, and what are our strategic responses?
- Given our *future* environmental and strategic choices, what technical and social competencies must employees demonstrate?

By facilitating these questions, HR professionals help general managers create a theory or point of view on competencies that leads to a set of employee standards. When general managers build competence models based on future customer expectations, they direct employee attention to knowing and doing the right things. The simplest test of the competence standard is to ask target or key customers, "If our employees lived up to these standards, would they inspire confidence from you in our firm?" When customers answer yes, the competence model is appropriate; if they answer no, it needs more work.

2. *Assess individuals and organizations.* With standards in place, employees can be assessed on the extent to which they meet or do not meet those standards. In recent years, most talent assessments evaluate both results and behavior. Talented employees deliver results in the right way. The right way is defined by the competence standards described in step 1. These behaviors can be self-assessed by the employee and others through a 360-degree review involving subordinates, peers, and supervisors. But to provide a holistic view of externally facing employees, they can also be evaluated by those outside the organization: suppliers, customers, investors, community leaders, and other external stakeholders. This shifts the 360-degree review to a 720 (360-degree internally + 360-degree externally = 720). This assessment helps the individual know what to do to improve and it also provides valuable input to the organization about how to design and deliver HR practices to upgrade talent. It also helps employees connect their work to the external constituents who ultimately judge the value of the company.

3. Invest in talent improvement. Individual and organizational gaps can be filled by investing in talent. In our work, we have found six kinds of investments that may be made to upgrade talent:

- *Buy:* Recruiting, sourcing, and securing new talent into the organization
- *Build:* Helping people grow through training on the job or through life experiences
- *Borrow:* Bringing knowledge into the organization through advisers or partners
- *Bound:* Promoting the right people into key jobs
- *Bounce:* Removing poor performers from their jobs and from the organization if they don't fit anywhere
- *Bind:* Retaining top talent

When HR professionals create choices in these six areas, they help individuals and organizations invest in future talent.

TOOL 5.1	*The Six Bs Overview*
	Obtain more information about the Six Bs and other resources that can help you align your HR practices with your business strategy.
	▶ *Go to www.TransformHR.com*

4. Follow up and track competence. Hoping for talent won't make it happen. Ultimately, you need talent measures that track how well individuals are developing their skills and how well the organization develops its talent bench. Individual employees can be tracked on their understanding of their next career step and their capacity to do it. Organizations can track the extent to which backups are in place for key positions. Leaders who are measured on how much money they contribute to their company can also be assessed on the extent to which they are talent producers rather than talent consumers.

These four basic steps will help HR professionals and general managers transform the quality of people or talent in their organization.

Commitment

Competence is not enough. Commitment means that employees are willing to devote their discretionary energy to the firm's success, responding to the basic employee value proposition the firm needs to offer: employees who give value to their organization should get value back from the organization. The ability to give value comes when employees are seen as able to deliver results in the right way.

Those employees who give value should get value back. In many studies of employee engagement, researchers have identified what employees get back from their work with the firm. Almost all consulting firms have engagement indexes that can be used as a pulse check to track employee engagement. Generally, these instruments suggest that employees are more committed when their organization offers them the following:

- *Vision:* A sense of direction or purpose
- *Opportunity:* An ability to grow, develop, and learn
- *Incentives:* A fair wage or salary for work done
- *Impact:* An ability to see the outcome or effect of work done
- *Community:* Peers, bosses, and leaders who build a sense of shared purpose, identity, and experience
- *Communication:* Knowing what is going on and why
- *Entrepreneurship or flexibility:* A range of choices about terms and conditions of work

When these seven dimensions exist in an organization, we suggest that employees have a VOI^2C^2E. They demonstrate their engagement by being at work on time, working hard, and doing what is expected of them. Commitment (not just satisfaction) can be measured through surveys or productivity indexes.

TOOL 5.2	*VOI²C²E Overview*
▣	Obtain more information about using the VOI²C²E model and other resources that can help you bolster and strengthen your employees such that they strengthen others.
	▶ *Go to www.TransformHR.com*

Contribution

We have found the next generation of employees may be competent (able to do the work) and committed (willing to do the work), but unless they are making a real contribution through the work (finding meaning and purpose in their work), then their interest in what they are doing diminishes and their talent wanes. One of our colleagues graduated from a top business school (a surrogate for competence) and got her ideal job, where she was willing to work very hard (commitment). But after about a year, she left. She still savored the job and was willing to work hard, but she felt that the job was not helping her meet her needs.

In recent years, many people are finding that the organizations where people's needs have traditionally been met (families, neighborhoods, hobby groups, churches) are faltering. As employees work longer hours and use technology that removes many work-life boundaries, companies need to learn how to help employees meet their needs. When people have their needs met through their organizations, they recognize that they are contributing and thus find abundance in their lives.

We have scoured findings from positive and developmental psychology, individual motivation, personal growth, high-performing teams, and organization theory to figure out what organizations and leaders can do to help employees find abundance. As a result, we have learned that employees will recognize their own contributions and perceive abundance in their work if their leaders help them answer these eight groups of questions:

- *Who am I?* How does employee identity meld with the company reputation?
- *Where am I going and why?* How can the organization help employees reach their own goals?
- *Who do I travel with?* How does the organization build a community of support so that employees are connected to one another?
- *How well do I practice spiritual disciplines?* How well does the organization build a positive work environment grounded in terms like *humility, service, forgiveness,* and *gratitude* rather than *hostility, self-interest,* and *politics?*
- *What challenges do I enjoy?* How does the organization help employees find challenges that are easy, enjoyable, and energizing?
- *How well can I access resources?* How does the organization help employees manage health, space, and financial requirements?
- *What are my sources of delight?* How does the organization help employees have fun?
- *How do I manage transitions?* How does the organization help employees manage the transitions associated with change?

When managers help employees find answers to these questions through their participation in the organization, the employees will find abundance in their lives and recognize that they are contributing to something that builds abundance in the world.

Summary of People Practices

In this talent equation, competence, commitment, and contribution are multiplicative, not additive. If one is missing, the other two will not replace it—a million times zero is still zero. Thus, a low score in competence will sharply reduce talent even when the employee is engaged and contributing. Talented employees must have skill, will, and purpose; they must be capable, committed, and contributing. Simply stated, competence deals with the head (being able), commitment with the hands and feet (being there), and contribution with the heart (simply being). HR leaders can engage their general managers to identify and improve each of these three dimensions to respond to the mandate for great talent.

Performance Practices: Flow of Performance Management

Performance practices turn desired outcomes into measurable goals and incentives that motivate people to reach those goals. The basic criteria for performance management are accountability, transparency, completeness, and equity. *Accountability* means that performance management practices should tie individual and team behavior and outcomes to clear goals. *Transparency* means that financial and nonfinancial rewards are understood and public. *Completeness* means that performance management practices cover the full range of behaviors and goals required for overall business success. *Equity* means that those who produce more receive more. When performance management practices are transformed according to these criteria, they help create value. Transformation of performance management practices can be done in four steps.

Step 1. Clarify Strategy and Priorities: Be Clear About What Is Wanted

Sometimes in the quest to have strategies that respond to complex business settings, leaders create strategic complexity. A first step in performance management is to be clear about an organization's strategy, performance priorities, and what it is trying to accomplish. Recently, we were invited to present on the third day of a three-day strategic off-site meeting. On day 1, the top team had reviewed their financial goals with over 150 PowerPoint slides. On day 2, they reviewed an equal number of slides about customers. When we started day 3, we were tempted to produce another 150 slides on people and organization. Instead, we asked each person to answer the basic question, "In twenty words or less, what is your strategy?" When pushed to simplify the complex financial and customer presentations, they could not reach a simple understanding and consensus. Before getting into HR practices to implement strategy, we found we needed to create strategic clarity. We call this creating a strategic story that offers a simple but clear narrative about what the company is trying to do.

Step 2. Set Standards: Define What to Measure

We often measure what is easy to measure rather than what is right to measure. Once strategy has been clarified, standards and measures can be created that match the strategy. To set the right standards, we have found the following questions useful:

- If this strategy is effective, we will see more of _____ and less of _____. Filling in the blanks is likely to lead you to measurable standards related to the strategy.
- How do we balance behavior and outcome standards for individuals and teams? This question helps balance the right standards given the strategy.
- What priority measures should we set? This question helps focus on the most important standards and measures given the strategy.
- What stretch targets should we set? This question sets standards for achievement in the future that provide more than what we have in the present.
- Who should set and monitor the standards? This question focuses on the process of setting the standards, which builds ownership of the standards set.

These questions help focus standards on the right issues and leads to ownership of those standards. A simple test of the right performance management standards is to test them with customers or investors, or both. If you went to these key external stakeholders and showed them the standards you have set, would they agree that they are more likely to buy products or invest in your firm because you meet these standards? If yes, your standards are measuring the right things; if not, your standards have missed the mark.

Step 3. Design Rewards: Build in Welcome and
Unwelcome Consequences

When someone meets your standards, both financial and nonfinancial rewards should follow. As Bruce Ellig points out, financial rewards have economic, psychic, and social implications, and the importance of each is different for every employee. Economically, money enables employees to develop a lifestyle that suits their needs. Psychically, money provides a feeling of personal worth and self-esteem. Socially, money determines a pecking order and a role and legitimacy in peer groups. Transforming financial rewards means making choices about these five types of income:

- *Short-term cash.* Base salary or on-the-spot cash compensation helps employees create and maintain a lifestyle. Base salary generally reflects tenure with the organization, job title, and performance.
- *Incentive-based cash.* These incentives are variable cash bonuses based on short-term or significant one-time performance contributions. The most common mid-term bonus is sales commission, but this type of reward has proven successful in a wide variety of job functions. Bonuses often make up from 10 percent to 150 percent of total cash compensation, putting enough pay at risk to reduce the common tendency to suboptimize for instant results.
- *Long-term equity.* Long-term equity in the form of stock options (the right to buy shares at a fixed price regardless of current market value) enables employees to gain wealth as the firm gains market value. The higher the stock price goes, the more an option is worth.

Nonfinancial rewards are also an important part of transforming performance management practices. These rewards include symbols of status (office space, title), workforce policies, benefits (health care and education), concierge services (transportation, car service), involvement in visible and important task forces, access to power and influence, and other benefits that don't put cash in the employees' pockets. When these nonfinancial rewards vary based on the extent to which an employee reaches standards, they have more impact than if they are randomly or uniformly applied.

Step 4. Follow up: Make Sure that Performance Management Endures

Follow-up—both feedback on prior activities and what Marshall Goldsmith admirably calls "feedforward" on what's needed—is critical to performance. Without honest self-assessment, no one can make progress. Here are some of the choices in providing follow-up:

- *Chat informally.* Informal conversations are often less onerous and more effective than a formal appraisal backed up by forms and procedures. In a casual setting—playing basketball or walking down the hall or over lunch— a comment about performance can raise the issue and lead to a productive conversation. This helps to make performance management a way of life in the company rather than (as our colleague Steve Kerr calls it) an experience of "unnatural acts in unnatural places."
- *Supply data.* People can't fix what they can't see. Provide charts and graphs that show revenues, profits, customer share, or other data both company-wide and as far as possible for individual work units. Offer specific examples of personal behaviors that need fixing.
- *Let people draw their own conclusions.* Data means more when the firm shares it and asks employees what they think. When employees assess the implications for themselves, they engage more fully and work to adjust results as needed. Questions often generate more thought than answers.
- *Explain the why, not the what.* When employees understand the why, they accept the what. Employees who understand why something needs to happen are more willing to work to make it happen than when they're simply told what to do.

- *Do it.* The most difficult part of follow-up is following up. HR's role is to make sure that providing feedback to employees is part of every supervisor's and team leader's performance appraisal.

In transforming performance practices, each of these four steps can be followed to upgrade performance management.

Information Practices: Flow of Information

Organizations must manage the inward flow of customer, shareholder, economic and regulatory, technological, and demographic information to make sure that employees recognize and adapt to external realities. They must also manage the internal flow of information across horizontal and vertical boundaries. HR professionals, with their sensitivity to people and processes, are ideally suited to assist with both information flows.

Information flow focuses on how you will communicate both inside and outside the organization. In transforming communication strategies, you will need to address five questions:

- *What is the message?* Be clear about the message that you want to communicate, which means keeping the message simple and focused.
- *Who should share the message?* Choose the most effective voice for the message, whether senior or local leaders, or both.
- *Who should receive the message?* Decide who needs to hear the message: employees at various levels of the organization, external stakeholders (customers, investors, communities, families of employees), or both.
- *When should the message be shared?* Timing matters; when employees read major announcements about the company in the press instead of directly from management, they feel disconnected from the company and tend to lose both morale and commitment.
- *How should we share the message?* Decide whether it's best to convey the ideas personally (in one-to-one interviews or small or large meetings) or impersonally (via the company website or video broadcasts).

As these five questions are addressed, information practices can be transformed to share consistent messages in meaningful ways. These practices spread information both inside the organization (top to bottom, bottom to top, and side to side) and outside the organization (to and from customers and investors).

Transforming information practices helps all stakeholders know both what is going on in an organization and why. Consistent messages shared redundantly will help build a shared agenda within an organization.

Work Practices: Flow of Work

Organizations must manage the flow of work from product or service demand through order fulfillment to make sure their obligations are met. To do so, they distribute goals to individuals and groups and set up job and organizational structures to integrate the varied output into a cooperative whole. They design processes for the work itself and set up a physical environment that promotes effective and efficient work. HR professionals are ideally suited to assist in all aspects of this process as well.

The first challenge involves organizational design. Here, the task is to make sure that the business strategy choices lead to organizational design options. We have clarified this in the chart shown in Figure 5.2 on the following page.

TOOL 5.3	*Strategy Assessment Worksheet*
	Download a copy of the Strategy Assessment Worksheet.
	▶ *Go to www.TransformHR.com*

This figure shows that strategy choices along the left side lead to organizational responses around single business units, while those on the right side lead to holding companies. Most companies are in the middle, with some form of diversification.

Figure 5.2 Strategy Choices and Structural Responses

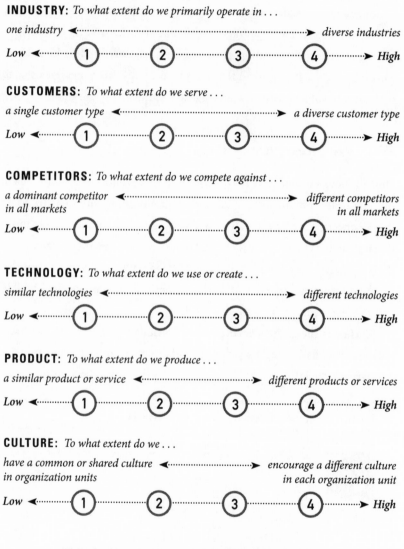

INDUSTRY: *To what extent do we primarily operate in . . .*

one industry ◄···► *diverse industries*

Low ◄·······**1**·············**2**·············**3**·············**4**·······► *High*

CUSTOMERS: *To what extent do we serve . . .*

a single customer type ◄·······································► *a diverse customer type*

Low ◄·······**1**·············**2**·············**3**·············**4**·······► *High*

COMPETITORS: *To what extent do we compete against . . .*

a dominant competitor in all markets ◄·······································► *different competitors in all markets*

Low ◄·······**1**·············**2**·············**3**·············**4**·······► *High*

TECHNOLOGY: *To what extent do we use or create . . .*

similar technologies ◄·······································► *different technologies*

Low ◄·······**1**·············**2**·············**3**·············**4**·······► *High*

PRODUCT: *To what extent do we produce . . .*

a similar product or service ◄·······································► *different products or services*

Low ◄·······**1**·············**2**·············**3**·············**4**·······► *High*

CULTURE: *To what extent do we . . .*

have a common or shared culture in organization units ◄·······································► *encourage a different culture in each organization unit*

Low ◄·······**1**·············**2**·············**3**·············**4**·······► *High*

The average of your scores leads to an organization response.

1   **2** **3** **4**

SINGLE BUSINESS UNIT   **RELATED DIVERSIFICATION**   **UNRELATED DIVERSIFICATION**   **HOLDING COMPANY**

Besides organizational design, HR transformation can focus on work processes, governance, and physical setting. Process improvements mean that HR can help reengineer business processes. These transformation efforts mean flow charting and streamlining how work is done in areas related to customers, suppliers, operations, or service. As discussed in Chapter 4, HR can help by facilitating discussions about the reduction of low-value-added work: redundant processes, inefficient meetings, meaningless paperwork and reports, and time spent waiting on approvals.

Governance refers to how decisions are made and implemented within the organization. This can involve issues related to top-down versus bottom-up patterns of decision making. It also refers to speed of decision making and whether decisions are made with a short- or long-term focus. HR can add value by helping management identify where decision making is best done. This involves finding answers to the following questions: Who has the relevant information? Who should have accountability for the decisions? Who should have accountability for implementing them? How do we involve these three groups of individuals in making key decisions?

Physical setting deals with space. At times, this is about walls, office space, and seating—features that can be modular and flexible or fixed and constrained. At other times, space questions involve lighting, pictures, colors, and other office arrangements. The physical space sends a message about your organization's culture and shapes the way people work together.

Collectively these four flows of HR work can be transformed to ensure that HR drives the results we talk about. Our experience is that often one or two of these domains are updated without attention to the rest of the model. This is like running on three flat tires and one full tire. The car won't drive well.

Process: Ways to Enhance HR Practices

There are three ways to transform HR practices so that they have the maximum impact: align, integrate, and innovate.

Align

For HR practices to have impact, they need to be aligned to the organization's strategy. Revisit the capabilities your organization needs to excel at. (See Chapter 3.) Do you have a clear and elegant statement of business strategy and the organizational capabilities that are required to make the strategy happen? The question then becomes, *To what extent does each of your HR practices support the development of these capabilities?* Given the pace of change and the effort required to change existing processes, it should be no surprise if some HR practices do not align as closely to the organization's strategy as you would like. One way to improve HR practices is to align the practices to the same criteria to make sure that they drive strategy through capability. If they are not clearly linked to those three things, either don't do them or else change them. That is where the real power comes from.

Integrate

When HR systems work together with a unified strategic focus to achieve the same outcomes, they have substantial impact on business results. If your HR practices are already aligned to the same criteria, integrating will be easier. Too often we find that organizations hired people for skills A, B, and C. Then the strategy shifted and they began training people to do D, E, and F. Meanwhile, they continued to pay people to do G, H, and I while communicating the importance of J, K, and L.

Integration means that your performance management practices, talent practices, compensation practices, communication practices, organizational design practices, and other HR practices present a consistent point of view and focus on how and why your organization manages its human assets. The idea is to ensure outside-in communications so that people maintain their line of sight to critical stakeholders. With that line of sight, performance management can make sure that people all understand what they need to do, how they need to do it, and that they need to do it. The degree to which they do what they need to do and the degree to which they do their work in the desired way will be part of the information covered in talent reviews. This information will also become input into their learning and development plans and their compensation expectations.

HR will have resources available to intervene in organizations that are struggling to meet performance expectations to help them develop skills or redesign structures or processes so that they will be able to meet those expectations. In other words, human resources will manage the time and energy of the people in the organization in as focused a manner as any other valuable and scarce resource. It does this by integrating all the practices that influence how people allocate their time and energy at work.

In influencing the contribution of the organization's human assets, HR practice results are based on synergy: the whole must be more than the parts. Our research shows a trend that concerns us: reward and talent practices are increasingly being separated. This trend is bound to lead to misalignments and disconnects that influence the ability of HR staff to maximize the contribution of the people in their organizations, and our research indicates that it is a real problem. As you look at which practices to address and how to manage those practices, be wary of reducing interdependencies in ways that improve efficiency but reduce overall contribution.

Transforming HR practices is about more than simply making incremental improvements to each one. In a fascinating study, Mark Huselid and his colleagues identified high-value HR practices and asked firms to rate their performance on those practices. He then correlated that data with financial performance and found three ranges where the performance of HR practices had a significant impact on the firm's overall performance. First, at the low end (between 0 and 20 out of 100), HR practices had a measurable positive impact on business performance because the business leaders and employees were thrilled to have HR support after living with no HR for so long. Second, in the midrange (from about 20 to 75 or 80), improvements in HR practices appeared to have little or no impact on business results. Third, once the range reached 75 or 80 and above, HR practices began to make a significant impact again. HR leaders must have the patience and resilience to develop an entire system of strategic HR practices and thus press through the barrier at 80 where HR has significant impact on business results.

Transformation of HR should not occur in isolation. The four domains we propose should be a coordinated and integrated approach rather than piecemeal and haphazard.

Innovate

To innovate, you need to keep abreast of the most recent HR practice innovations in your industry and in the broader HR community. What are your rising competitors doing and how? What are leading thinkers finding out about how to drive impact with practice? Both practical and theoretical innovations should be examined against the capabilities you are trying to drive: Will this innovation make this HR practice more effective in building customer connectivity? Speed? Efficiency? If so, you should adapt (not adopt) the innovation—use it in a form designed to fit your culture and your goals. Sometimes these innovations will not work out. That is the risk of innovation. But "fast failure" is not bad if you learn from it and adjust.

Making the Change: Transforming HR Practices

You can use the road map in Figure 5.1 in one of two ways, by starting a focus either on content (the four categories of HR practice) or on process (the four ways to enhance HR practices). Resist the temptation to focus on just one (or a few) of the cells, without paying attention to the rest. All twelve cells matter.

In an HR transformation effort, it is important to identify which practices and processes will contribute most to achieving the desired outcomes of the initiative. Begin by compiling a list of practices within each work cluster. Assess each practice using an instrument like the HR Practice Assessment Worksheet at www.TransformHR.com. Identify the practices that will quickly move you to the HR practice impact points discussed above, and ensure those practices receive the focus they need during the HR transformation.

To transform HR practices, engage your internal organization, your process redesign group, and your HR leadership team. Many companies have found it useful to identify and retain an external consultant to focus on the planning process so that the HR team can focus on content related to the plan. Map the core HR practices, create a master HR systems design plan, create design recommendations for each practice, establish desired outcomes and measures for each affected practice, create breakthrough practice design concepts, align the practice with other HR and corporate practices, consolidate the design recommendations and create implementation plans, and implement the changes in concert with people and department changes. Finally, ensure that each HR practice—whether addressed in the transformation or not—has clear measures in place that allow you to continually monitor the contribution the practices make to critical organizational outcomes and help identify ways to improve them.

TOOL 5.4	*Transforming HR Practices*
▶	Listen to Jon Younger describe how he has helped many HR departments transform their practices to align with customer needs. In particular, listen to Jon's unique perspective on how to link talent to customers.
	▶ *Go to www.TransformHR.com*

CHAPTER 6

UPGRADE HR PROFESSIONALS

6

Ultimately, HR transformation depends on the quality of HR professionals. Given the challenges of understanding the full business context (Phase 1), defining important business related outcomes (Phase 2), and redesigning the HR department and state-of-the-art HR practices (Phase 3), the bar has been raised for HR professionals. The competencies that were all HR professionals once needed are no longer sufficient in the new world of HR challenges. What it took to succeed in human resources in the past has changed with the emerging challenges that we address in this book. In this chapter, we enlarge upon the four-step model for building competencies introduced in Chapter 5:

- *Step 1: Articulate a theory or set a standard.* Prepare a statement of what standards are required for HR professionals to be successful.
- *Step 2: Assess individuals and organizations.* Establish a methodology for determining how well HR professionals do or do not meet the required standards.
- *Step 3: Invest in talent improvement.* Prepare a portfolio of development activities intended to upgrade HR professionals.
- *Step 4: Follow up and track competence.* Develop a methodology to integrate the changes required for HR professionals to respond to increased expectations.

Following this model, you can learn to build the competencies of HR professionals so that they can respond to increased expectations.

Step 1: Theory and Standards

The key question here is, What standards are required for HR professionals to be successful?

Defining what it means to be a successful HR professional has been one of our primary pursuits for more than twenty years. In that time, we have discovered a number of ways to determine the essentials of effectiveness. We have talked about HR roles (the identity and reputation of an HR professional), HR activities (day-to-day work that HR professionals do), and HR competencies (knowledge, skill, and abilities of HR professionals). We believe that the roles and activities combine to form the competencies for HR professionals, as sketched in Figure 6.1.

Figure 6.1 Background of HR Effectiveness

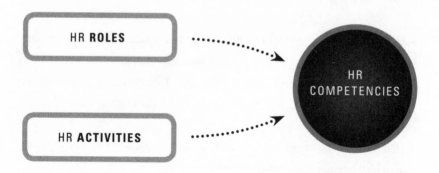

We recommend that companies focus their HR professional development on HR competencies, which we believe integrate the roles and activities. However, we have been in some companies that prefer to define effective HR by roles or activities. If a company wants to increase the reputation of its HR professionals, roles might be a good starting point. If a company wants to improve the day-to-day work of HR, activities might be a good starting point. But in either case, we believe that the HR competencies we suggest integrate both roles and activities. Thus, we focus on defining effective HR through HR competencies that we have studied and assessed.

In this chapter, we briefly discuss the roles and activities, then focus on the competencies required for HR professionals.

HR Roles

We have evolved our definition of the roles for HR professionals that deliver value, but the basic premises have stayed the same. A role represents an identity or image of an individual as seen by that individual and by others. This concept can be made practical in the completion of the following phrase: *To deliver value as an HR professional, I must be a* _____.

In our original work for the book *HR Champions*, we defined four roles, each tied to an outcome of what HR professionals should deliver:

- The *employee champion* focuses attention on helping employees develop competence, generate commitment, and discover contribution.
- The *administrative expert* delivers HR practices with efficiency.
- The *change agent* helps the organization adapt to new conditions.
- The *strategic partner* aligns HR practices with business strategies.

All four roles must be played in an HR organization for HR professionals to be effective, yet an individual HR contributor may be a master of one role while being only sympathetic to and supportive of the other three. Some HR leaders may be moving HR toward the strategic and change roles and ignoring the employee champion and administrative expert roles, which threaten HR credibility. When the basics are not being done well, strategic impact is short-lived.

As business conditions have evolved over the last decade, so have the roles of HR also evolved. We thus have morphed these original four roles, shown in the first column of Table 6.1, to the five shown in the second column.

Table 6.1 Evolution of HR Roles

LATE 1990s	LATE 2000s	EVOLUTION OF THINKING
Employee Champion	Employee Advocate (EA)	Employees are increasingly critical to the success of organizations. EA focuses on today's employee.
	Human Capital (HC) Developer	HC developer focuses on how employees prepare for the future.
Administrative Expert	Functional Expert	HR practices are central to HR value. Some HR practices are delivered through administrative efficiency (such as technology), and others through policies, menus, and interventions, expanding the functional expert role.
Change Agent	Strategic Partner	Being a strategic partner has multiple dimensions: business expert, change agent, knowledge manager, and consultant. Being a change agent represents only part of the strategic partner role.
Strategic Partner	Strategic Partner	The view has expanded to encompass the dimensions once attributed to either the strategic partner or the change agent roles.
	Leader	The sum of the first four roles equals leadership, but being an HR leader also has implications for leading the HR function, integrating work of other functions, ensuring corporate governance, and monitoring the HR community.

Source: Dave Ulrich, *Human Resource Champions*

HR professionals are *employee advocates*, charged with making sure the employer-employee relationship is one of reciprocal value. Besides advocating for employees today, they build the future workforce as *human capital developers*. HR professionals are also *functional experts*, designing and delivering

HR practices that ensure individual ability and create organization capability. As *strategic partners*, they help line managers at all levels reach their goals. HR professionals bring business, change, consulting, and learning know-how to their partnership with line managers, so that together they create value. And to tie it all together, they must be genuine *leaders*—credible both to their own functions and to those outside. When these five roles are played within the HR department, HR professionals have more impact.

HR Actions

Day-to-day HR work focuses on what HR professionals might do to fill the multiple events on their calendars. The calendar may be filled with individual or team meetings, site visits, problem-solving sessions, or personal reflection time. In each of these forums, we have found that HR professionals perform four activities: coaching, architecting, designing and delivering, and facilitating.

Coaching

In recent years, coaching has become a movement within HR, even a fad. HR professionals (and outside consultants) coach individual business leaders to reflect on and improve their performance. We see two distinct but connected models of coaching: behavior and results. Behavior-based coaching focuses on what leaders do and how they do it. Results-based coaching focuses on helping leaders clarify the results they hope to deliver. In day-to-day interactions, HR professionals coach those they work with by gaining credibility, listening carefully, advising wisely, and offering direct and candid observations.

Architecting

Home or building architects turn lifestyles and life experiences into tangible and durable structures in which people live. As organizational architects, HR professionals turn general and generic ideas into tangible and durable blueprints for organizational action. They continually look for the strategic agenda of the firm and try to envision its implications for an organizational agenda.

They perform organizational diagnoses by adapting an organizational model to business strategy. In daily work, HR professionals often deal with immediate challenges and crises, but they should always be aware of the broader organizational architecture they are building.

Designing and Delivering

HR professionals design and deliver HR practices. As discussed in Chapter 5, HR professionals align, integrate, and innovate HR practices that will contribute to company success. To design and deliver HR practices, HR professionals need to be current in theory, research, and practices. They need to be able to adapt general principles to specific circumstances. Daily HR work is often done in short-term bursts and firefighting, but when this work is done through systematic HR practices, the efficiency and effectiveness of HR become more sustainable.

Facilitating

As facilitators, HR professionals are attuned to the processes of macro and micro change. At the micro level, they facilitate team meetings and planning sessions. At the macro level, they facilitate large-scale system change. In many organizations, the aspirations for change are greater than the actions of change. Making change happen in any organization requires not only focus of what should be changed but also management of the process of getting acceptance and support for the change. As facilitators, HR professionals can help negotiate not only what should be changed but how to go about making the desired change happen. In daily interactions, HR professionals should have an agenda for how the culmination of diverse activities keeps the organization moving toward a longer-term success.

As HR professionals coach, architect, design and deliver, and facilitate, they transform themselves from reactive staff followers into proactive business contributors. While they must deal with daily demands, they should also make progress in contributing to the broader organizational success.

HR's Professional Competencies

We have combined the work on HR roles and activities into a cohesive framework for HR competencies. In the last 20 years, we have regularly assessed the competencies that make HR successful through the Human Resource Competency Study (HRCS). In the most recent round of this study, conducted in 2007, we have identified the competencies required of HR professionals based on data from just over 10,000 people around the world. Our findings are summarized in Figure 6.2.

Figure 6.2 *Key Attributes of HR*

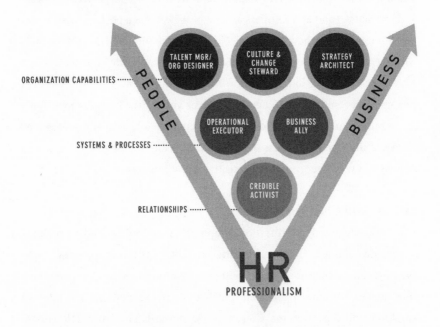

This figure shows that to be successful as an HR professional requires managing both people (being attuned to the human dimensions of a company) and business (mastering the requirements of the business). Within these two dimensions, our research has identified six competence domains that lead to effective HR professionalism.

TOOL 6.1	*HR Competencies Overview*
▶	Over the last 20 years, Dave Ulrich and Wayne Brockbank have gathered the world's largest database on HR competencies that positively impact business success. Listen to Wayne describe the results of the latest round of data collection and the implications for HR professionals.
	▶ *Go to www.TransformHR.com*

Credible Activist

The most effective HR professionals are both credible (respected, admired, and listened to) and active (offers a point of view, takes a position, challenges assumptions). Some have called this "HR with an attitude." HR professionals who are credible but not activists are admired but have little impact. Activists who are not credible have ideas that no one implements. Credibility moves you up the people axis, and activism moves you up the business axis. Both are required for transformational HR. As credible activists, HR professionals create sustainable business outcomes as they link the people and business dimensions with energy, insight, sensitivity, and impact.

Culture and Change Steward

The most effective HR professionals appreciate, articulate, and help shape a company's culture. Culture is a pattern of activities rather than any single event. Ideally, this culture starts with clarity around external expectations (firm identity or brand) and then translates these expectations into internal employee and organizational behaviors. As stewards of culture, HR professionals respect the past culture and also help to shape a new culture. They coach managers in how their actions reflect and drive culture, weave cultural standards into HR practices and processes, and make culture real to employees. Additionally, successful HR professionals facilitate change by helping make culture happen and by developing disciplines to make change happen throughout the organization. This may include implementation of strategy, projects, or initiatives. They help turn what is known into what is done.

Talent Manager and Organization Designer

The most effective HR professionals master theory, research, and practice in both talent management and organizational design. Talent management focuses on competency requirements and how individuals enter and move up, across, or out of the organization. Organizational design focuses on how a company embeds capability (for example, collaboration or innovation) into the structure, processes, and policies that shape the way it works. HR professionals should ensure that the company's means of talent management and organizational capabilities are aligned with strategy, integrated with each other, and working effectively and efficiently. HR is not just about talent or organization, it is also about the two of them together. Good talent without a supporting organization will not be sustained, and a good organization will not deliver results without talented individuals with the right competencies in critical roles.

Strategy Architect

The most effective HR professionals have a vision for how the organization can perform and win in the marketplace, now and in the future. HR professionals play an active part in the establishment of the overall strategy to deliver on this vision by being an active participant in creating strategy. They also turn strategy into HR practices that culminate in organizational capabilities. They ensure that leader behaviors throughout the organization match the strategy. They help articulate how the strategy bridges employees inside and customers outside. They manage the process of who is involved in shaping and sharing the strategy.

Operational Executor

The most effective HR professionals execute the operational aspects of managing people and organization. Policies need to be drafted, adapted, and implemented. Employees also have many administrative needs (for example, to be hired, trained, relocated, and paid), and HR professionals ensure that these basic needs are efficiently dealt with through technology, shared services, or outsourcing. This operational work of HR ensures credibility if executed flawlessly and grounded in the consistent application of policies. HR professionals continually solicit and receive feedback from employees on the accuracy, speed, and responsiveness of all HR administrative processes and practices.

Business Ally

Businesses succeed by setting goals and objectives that respond to external opportunities and threats and executing plans of action that achieve those ends. HR professionals should contribute to the success of a business by knowing the social context or setting in which their business operates. They also know how the business makes money, which we call the *value chain of the business*: who customers are, why they buy the company's products or services, and how the company has organized itself to respond to customer requirements. Finally, they have a good understanding of the internal business processes, of the value proposition of the various functions (finance, marketing, research and development, engineering), and of what these functions must accomplish and how they work together, so that they can help the business organize to make money. They can pass a business literacy test of how the business operates.

Summary: Standards for HR Professional Success

In transforming HR professionals, the first step is to be clear about what is expected for success in the field. By considering roles and activities, we can specify six competencies that define the standards for HR professionals. These six domains of HR competency define what it takes to be an effective HR professional as well as the expectations and standards for high-impact HR professionals.

TOOL 6.2	*HR Competencies Research*
	Download a concise summary of the RBL / University of Michigan HR Competencies study as well as the first chapter of the *HR Competencies* (2008) book.
	▶ *Go to www.TransformHR.com*

Step 2: Assessment

The key question here is, How do we determine if HR professionals meet the standards expected of them?

Once standards have been set, HR professionals need to know how well they meet those standards. There are informal and formal ways of assessing performance against standards. Informally, good HR professionals constantly seek feedback. They see how others respond to them; they ask for suggestions on how they can improve in specific HR skill areas; they do thoughtful self-reflection to see what works and what does not. HR professionals should look for patterns of how they are perceived by others. Some of the following questions might help you with your informal assessment of your own skills:

- What are some of the common challenges I run into when trying to accomplish my work?
- How do people generally respond to me?
- What work do I find easy, energizing, and enjoyable?
- What work do I get excited about doing? What work do I avoid by procrastinating, avoiding, and postponing?
- What do I need to do less of and what do I need to do more of to add greater value to my internal and external customers?
- Who are the people I trust most? Am I willing to ask them for suggestions for how I can improve?
- How do I respond when I receive feedback? Am I able to process the information without becoming defensive?

Honestly looking in a mirror and seeing what is really there helps HR professionals know their strengths and weaknesses.

HR professionals can also seek formal feedback on how they are doing. Some of this assessment may come from personality and other self-awareness tests. Access to self-assessments may come from personal experiences (for example, going online to gain access to personality assessments) or from formal company interventions (for example, doing a personal assessment as part of a corporate initiative). One key we have found for using these personal assessments effectively is to not over- or underreact. Overreaction would be to immediately change behaviors and actions without considering how well the findings apply to the immediate situation. Underreaction would be to discount the information with equal lack of thought. It is also important to be aware that spontaneous self-assessment is often flawed. In general, we can identify our strengths better than our weaknesses.

Thus, it is important to receive feedback from a variety of different sources, in what are often called 360-degree feedback processes. Most HR professionals have done a 360-degree review where they receive feedback from diverse stakeholders: peers, subordinates, supervisors, and clients. Seeing patterns in these data can help HR professionals learn how they are seen by others, where they are strong, and where they need improvement. For example, we coached one HR professional who moved into a leadership role but continued to spend time with subordinates rather than peers. The 360-degree feedback was higher from subordinates than from peers or supervisors. With this information, the new executive was able to understand the behaviors required in the new role.

Here are some of the lessons we have learned in receiving 360-degree feedback:

- Look for patterns in the data, and avoid concentrating too much on specific events.
- Do 360-degree reviews at intervals so that you can compare yourself with yourself and monitor personal improvements over time.
- Don't try to guess who said what.
- Focus on one or two specific behaviors you can improve.
- Do 360-degree assessments that focus on HR, not just generic leadership assessments.
- Whenever possible, compare yourself to larger populations of HR professionals to see how you are doing relative to the broader HR community.

It is also useful in looking at 360-degree data to evaluate the predisposi-tions of the overall HR community. Sometimes, HR departments have pat-terns that show up in regular 360-degree reviews. In one company, we found that almost none of the HR professionals were business allies. The entire HR community scored lower than the national norms for business knowledge. When we shared this data with the senior HR team, they decided to engage in a business literacy program for the entire HR community.

TOOL 6.3	*HR Competencies Assessments*
① ② ③ ④	Ensure that you are focused on developing the right skills for your HR professionals by assessing them and then comparing data from your organization with global norms. Download a sample report of the RBL HR Competencies 360 Assessment.
	▶ *Go to www.TransformHR.com*

We have also done more intense behavior-based assessments where a trained interviewer collects data on an HR professional's behavior from the individual and several targeted stakeholders. This behavioral intervention is more intense, with an initial interview with the HR professional lasting between two and six hours. Interviewers focus on the patterns of behavior that the individuals have demonstrated throughout their lives, with an emphasis on how they have succeeded and what has caused them to stumble. Similar information is collected face-to-face from between 10 and 30 stakeholders, with a focus on key strengths and the one barrier that is doing most to restrict the individual's success. Once the data have been collected, assessors compile a series of reports that outline the individual's career story, highlight strengths and development needs, and provide a highly tailored development plan. Such a plan may include a wide variety of recommendations, from daily read-ing of the *Financial Times* to a vacation in China to a specific new business assignment where the individual can address particular development needs.

These rigorous assessments are generally reserved for evaluating the readiness of executives who are candidates for significant senior roles or for developing high-potential leaders fairly early in their careers. Participants in this type of assessment often describe the process as the most beneficial development experience of their careers.

In any of these assessment efforts, it is important that the recipients of the information seek to remain nondefensive, open, and willing to change. If others give feedback that is never acted upon, they will eventually quit giving feedback. It is also important to see patterns of perception. The recipients ultimately control the data and determine their own improvement agenda. We suggest they focus on one or two important changes that others will notice.

If you are fortunate enough to receive such an assessment, see if you can identify a gap between the standards for what effective HR professionals know and do and the quality of your own awareness and action on those standards. Bear in mind that receiving and acting on such information is an ongoing, career-long process. Regardless of your career stage or the level of your position, there is always room for important progress.

Step 3: Investment

The key question here is, How do we create learning opportunities to develop our HR professionals?

After a gap has been identified—both for each individual and for the department as a whole—the next step is investment. Investing in HR professionals means allocating time and resources to upgrading their skills. In learning research, it was reported at the 21st Annual Society of Industrial and Organizational Psychology (SIOP) conference in 2006, scholars have found that about 50 percent of what we are able to do comes from nature and 50 percent from nurture. As we apply this metaphor to building HR capability, *nature* refers to hiring HR professionals with the required knowledge, skills, and abilities; *nurture* refers to developing HR professionals with the required knowledge, skills, and abilities. Companies must begin by hiring the right HR professionals—and by removing the wrong ones, if they recognize past hiring mistakes. Hiring the right people means making sure that those who interview potential candidates use a rigorous interview process and screen candidates against a common set of criteria. But even with rigorous hiring processes, some HR professionals won't be effective. Screening efforts are not flawless, circumstances change, and some people don't evolve into new expectations. Therefore, removing poorly performing HR professionals becomes a critical strategy to upgrade the company's HR community. In removing people, it is important to make sure that the criteria for performance are clear, that people all know how they are doing against those standards, that leaders act boldly when someone consistently fails to meet the standards, and that the person is treated fairly in the outplacement process. Removing poor performers sends a message to others that poor performance will not be tolerated. It also builds confidence in the current leader among high-performing employees. We have found some line managers discredit HR because HR asks them to make tough hiring and firing decisions but won't apply the same standards to itself. Investing in human resources means screening and outplacing with rigor.

In addition, investing in HR means nurturing HR professionals to higher levels of professionalism and performance by providing development experiences. We have found three approaches to developing HR professionals: job experience, training experience, and life experience.

Job Experience

The most powerful way to learn is by experience. We learn by doing. Several approaches might be used to provide on-the-job learning. Moving someone into a new job can provide a powerful learning opportunity; moving from a center of expertise to a business unit job or being assigned to work on an innovative business project is bound to stretch existing skills. We worked with one company that had sold a business and gained a sizable sum of cash. The HR leader assigned some high-potential HR professionals to a special task force to build a merger or acquisition checklist. At the time the assignment was made, no specific mergers or acquisitions were being actively considered. Nonetheless, the head of HR realized that with a sizable hoard of cash, the company was likely to make a merger or acquisition move in the near future. The team of high potentials came up with a thoughtful and rigorous method for assessing people and organizational issues as part of a comprehensive merger and acquisition strategy. When the acquisition opportunity arrived, the information from the high-potential team was immediately useful. In the process, the HR high potentials learned a great deal about business issues that were important for their own success and that of their employer.

Here are some additional work experiences that we have seen help HR professionals broaden and deepen their experiences:

- Make a line-to-staff move or vice versa.
- Coach or mentor someone else.
- Be assigned to profit-and-loss accountability early in a career and then move to successively larger assignments.
- Choose to take international assignments with different cultural experiences.
- Work in a turnaround situation.
- Be charged with a significant portion of a merger or acquisition deal.
- Do a cross-functional rotation.
- Participate in a customer internship.
- Work for a different boss.
- Do a series of customer interviews.
- Attend an investor conference and share company information with investors.
- Participate on project teams that are add-ons to the present work assignment.

In addition, to optimally develop HR professionals, it is important to consider geographical location, alternative HR roles, and industry type when making job assignments. Locating high-potential HR professionals in non-traditional markets helps them learn the dynamics of global business. Global experience can take the form of a temporary project or a permanent assignment, but good HR professionals must appreciate the subtlety of managing in global settings. It is also possible to consider using alternative HR roles as a means for HR professional development: moving individuals among corporate, centers of expertise, embedded HR, and service center roles. We have found that careers in HR are more of a mosaic than linear. HR professionals can also develop important business knowledge and skills by being exposed to a variety of unique business challenges (for example, start-ups and mature businesses or consumer and industrial sales).

Work or job experience can be transformational for HR professionals. It offers them new opportunities, challenges, and insights. It also tests their ability to learn and adapt, which becomes a prediction of their future potential.

Training Experience

All too often, HR professionals and departments are so caught up in *delivering* training that they are the last to receive formal training in how to upgrade their roles. To ensure that training investments have maximum impact, the following measures make a big difference:

- *Connect HR training not just to strategy but to customers and investors.* We worked in one company that included customers and investors in the training of its HR professionals. When faculty teach, participants learn; when line managers teach, participants do; when customers and investors teach, participants do the right things.
- *Prepare an integrated model for HR development.* We have seen training as a "parade of stars" where individual presenters are dynamic and engaging but

the overall program does not offer an integrated view for those being developed. Make sure that the modules flow from one to another. Ensure that the learning whole is greater than the sum of the parts.

- *Consider the training as an experience, not an event.* An experience means preliminary work, application, and follow-up, not just the time in the training classroom.
- *Bring real work into the training program in the form of team or individual action-learning projects.* We have found it useful to set specific revenue or cost-saving targets for such projects.
- *Make sure that training has analytics.* This might mean a 360-degree feedback session for the individual participants or business problems that can be solved with the skills that should be learned in the program.

Effective training can be a powerful source of development for HR professionals striving to become more strategic. We have had remarkable success in training HR professionals to increase their impact on business results. In one company, Ryan Quinn and Wayne Brockbank report, the perception of HR's impact on business results increased 120 percent as a result of the HR training intervention.

We have seen three different forums for HR training programs. Each has its own strengths and weaknesses. *In-house training programs* provide the opportunity to develop a unified, business-focused HR paradigm in the company's HR community. The training is customized to the company's specific business situation and implementation challenges can be thoroughly addressed and overcome. *University-based public programs* are designed to help individual HR professionals enhance their personal knowledge and skills. The presence of people from different companies provides exposure to a wide variety of HR practices from different industries and different global regions. And an emerging *hybrid* of the two traditional approaches encourages a consortium of companies to send small teams of HR professionals—five to seven people from a company—

company—to a program. This latter approach provides the opportunity for extensive best-practice sharing and team-based application projects.

Life Experience

Learning also stems from personal choices. This might include building a personalized reading program where HR professionals regularly read, report, and apply key concepts from leading thinkers. Learning through listening can be accomplished by attending conferences where emerging HR trends are presented. As Michael Lombardo and Robert Eichinger note, learning by observing goes on constantly for those who are inquisitive and seek new ideas. Best-practice benchmarking allows HR professionals to compare themselves to others whom they admire. They can observe what other companies do and then adapt what they see to their respective contexts.

HR professionals can develop by experimenting with new behaviors. You can try out new behaviors, observe how others respond, and make appropriate adjustments. If you are predisposed to be quiet, you can practice speaking up; if you tend to overanalyze numbers before making decisions, you can experiment with making spot decisions. It helps to be willing to take risks—to look stupid and not get something right the first time—as insisting on being right at the beginning is often the main barrier to learning. When you try something new, you may not succeed at first, but if you don't try new behaviors, you will atrophy.

Keeping a learning journal helps you see how you are progressing and what you are learning. Be in a constant inquisitive mode to see what could be done better. When you visit a restaurant, grocery store, shopping mall, or government agency, ask yourself, "What could be done better here?" These personal learning strategies help you develop a learning attitude and mindset. Learning-by-doing-and-reflecting has long been recognized as a powerful way to enhance personal skill development.

Summary: Learning Opportunities for HR Professionals

HR knowledge has a half-life. That is, 50 percent of what HR professionals should know and do changes every few years. To stay current and even ahead of the HR knowledge curve, HR professionals need to invest in themselves at work, in training, and in their personal lives.

TOOL 6.4	*Strategic HR Professional Development*
▶	Effective development of HR professionals involves interventions in three key categories: work experience, life experience, and formal training/mentoring. Learn from leading global organizations as Justin Allen shares best practices in sustainable leadership development.
	▶ *Go to www.TransformHR.com*

Step 4: Measurement and Follow-up

The key question here is, How do we measure and follow up to make sure that ideas are sustained?

The final step in any talent improvement model is measuring and following up. Measurement means tracking the quality of the HR professionals and of the investments to develop the HR professionals. We have worked with a number of companies that have consistently done HR 360-degree reviews to track the quality of their HR professionals. Having a baseline of HR performance and then regularly benchmarking against that baseline allows HR leaders to present progress to their business leaders. In addition, it is important to test the extent to which HR investments yield results. Do the job assignments help people prepare for future career opportunities? Do the HR training experiences help people learn new ideas and behave differently? Do the development experiences translate into the creation of key organizational capabilities that, in turn, translate into substantially greater business results? Does encouragement of personal learning help HR professionals broaden their experience and make them more able to meet the standards expected of them?

Measurement and follow-up mean that HR transformation should not just be about the development of HR professionals. It also requires that HR development should be part of HR performance management, that the goals and processes of the HR transformation are clearly and comprehensively communicated, and that HR work is optimally organized to deliver value. When all of the four HR practice areas discussed in Chapter 5 (people, performance, information, work) are applied to transforming HR professionals, the development initiative becomes integrated and more sustainable.

Conclusion

This chapter talks about transforming the quality of HR professionals. The four-step model for talent management in general can be adapted for upgrading all HR professionals within your organization or for improving your individual HR skills. We have worked with a number of chief HR officers who wanted to upgrade their HR professionals. Using the HR competency model we have generated, they have combined a number of individual HR audits to determine the overall quality of their HR professionals. With this information, they have created an HR academy where HR professionals learn how to create value. The outcome of these development experiences is that HR professionals have a dramatic increase in how they are perceived to deliver value to their organization.

At a more personal level, HR professionals can use these ideas to improve their skills. An emerging HR leader named Jenna aspired to delivering HR excellence. As she anticipated what she hoped to accomplish in her career, she recognized that she needed to identify and develop her personal competencies. She studied and learned the competence model we developed. She asked her associates how well she performed in each of the six domains. She prioritized the areas where she needed to improve the most and created a personal development plan for her improvement. With little public fanfare, her boss, clients, peers, and subordinates began to recognize her personal progress. With renewed confidence, Jenna began to receive increasingly complex assignments and responsibilities, and she anticipated success in her career.

For either the HR department as a whole or for individual HR professionals, when there is a clear set of expectations and standards, HR professionals may assess themselves against those standards, invest in their future, and measure their development and follow up on it. As a result, they are transformed in ways that help them contribute to their organization's long-term success.

Phase 4

HR ACCOUNTABILITY

CHAPTER 7

SHARE ACCOUNTABILITY FOR THE TRANSFORMATION 7

A successful process of HR transformation involves the right people at the right time in the right way. We call this Phase 4, but it is a critical feature of all phases. The importance of involvement in successful change management is well established. We know from decades of social-psychological research that people are more likely to be committed to activities or decisions in which they are involved. This has particularly important—and not entirely obvious—implications for HR leaders and professionals engaged in transformation. If HR professionals plan the transformation in a vacuum, others whose perspectives are needed during planning or whose commitment is needed during implementation are apt to resist the changes required of them; they will be less likely to support the more controversial or difficult elements of the plan, and they certainly will be less supportive or helpful as problems or challenges arise in the course of implementation.

Four groups of stakeholders should be involved with the HR transformation:

- *HR leaders and professionals:* Design the process and work to implement the transformation
- *Line managers:* Make sure the transformation aligns to business goals and work with HR to implement the transformation
- *External customers and investors:* Guide the HR transformation for relevance
- *Consultants and advisers:* Offer frameworks and insights developed by others, and point out potholes that others have stumbled into

HR Leaders and Professionals

Ultimately, HR transformation depends on the quality of HR professionals and their relationships with line managers. If they cannot respond to the increased expectations raised by transformation, they will quickly lose credibility and be relegated to second-tier status. Four roles are important to this process: the chief HR officer (CHRO), the HR leadership team, the head of HR for HR, and HR professionals.

Chief HR Officer (CHRO)

The leader of any organization sets the direction and tone for that organization. The CHRO needs to sponsor the HR transformation. This means allocating money, time, and talent to the transformation effort. The sponsor also needs to keep key stakeholders (line managers, the board of directors) informed of progress and to hold those doing the day-to-day work of HR transformation accountable. The CHRO should initiate, take the lead in the design, and monitor the transformation plan, making sure that this plan starts with business context (phase 1); defines deliverables and outcomes (phase 2); specifies changes for the HR department, practices, and people (phase 3); and implements changes. Finally, the CHRO should ensure that robust measurements are in place to credibly and accurately monitor progress. Ensuring that credible HR professionals are involved requires CHRO sponsorship. Like all transformations, HR transformation will have its share of ups and downs. Steady and unflinching support is critical when leading the effort.

Often a new head of HR from outside the company has an easier time advocating HR transformation than a current or internally promoted HR head. Those who built an HR agenda are less likely to be willing to undo and transform it. While a new external CHRO may bring new views and vitality to an HR transformation, however, an outsider also has to work hard to understand and build on earlier work. An in-place or internally promoted head of HR can better accomplish transformation by making sure that it is grounded in business context (phase 1) with clear outcomes (phase 2).

HR Leadership Team

Most HR heads construct a leadership team. Usually the team consists of the HR leaders for businesses or key geographic units, the heads of centers for expertise, and the shared services or transactional (or HR operations) HR leader. This team may be called the leadership team, the steering committee, the HR cabinet, or something similar. Whatever the name, this group's collective support for HR transformation is critical and should not be overlooked or assumed.

HR for HR

In many large companies, the champions of the HR transformation are the individuals charged with providing HR services for HR professionals. These individuals are generally seasoned HR professionals who have worked in increasingly responsible HR positions in both businesses units and centers of expertise. The individuals in these roles very often have an excellent understanding of how the business operates and makes money. They need to have a strong reputation among HR professionals who look to them for guidance and among business leaders whose support may hang on their credibility.

As the head of the HR transformation team, they draft the HR transformation plan and make sure that milestones (discussed in Chapter 8) are in place to make and monitor progress. They are also responsible for facilitating discussions of how to organize the HR department so that center-of-expertise and embedded HR professionals collaborate to deliver value (Chapter 4). They help contract for technology to deliver administrative processes efficiently. They supervise HR practice audits to determine which practices (people, performance, information, and work) should receive priority (Chapter 5). They ensure that these practices align with strategy, integrate with each other, and address matters the organization genuinely needs to deal with. They are responsible for defining the standards for what makes an effective HR professional in their organizations and creating a process to assess HR professionals against those standards (Chapter 6). They take the lead in investing in HR development experiences and training. They are actively involved in the succession planning process and promotions to key HR positions throughout the company. They manage the processes necessary to make change happen. They work to create the future of HR, rather than relying on past successes to maintain their place in the organization.

HR Professionals

Even when sponsored by the CHRO and championed by the head of HR for HR, an HR transformation must be enacted and lived by HR professionals throughout the organization if it is to have any prospect of success. HR professionals who embrace transformation recognize that their personal success is linked to that of the HR transformation. This means letting go of past behaviors, learning new roles, practicing new activities, and mastering key competencies. Letting go of the past means realizing that, as Marshall Goldsmith says, "What got you here won't get you there."

In almost every HR transformation we have experienced, some proportion (often about a fifth) of the HR professionals were early adopters, people who were primed and ready for the transformation and eager to get started when given the chance. It is important to identify these innovators and sponsor them, support them, and broadcast to others what they are doing. An equal proportion are laggards who cannot let go of the past and will never make the transformation. These individuals also need to be identified early and moved out or aside so that the transformation can proceed smoothly. The largest group of HR professionals are probably in the middle of the pack: willing to consider the transformation but not sure how it affects them or how to make it happen. For this group, the CHRO and champion of the transformation need to build the business case for the transformation (phase 1), clearly define the deliverables (phase 2), and create a blueprint for changing HR departments and practices (phase 3). HR professionals in this group also need rigorous and regular feedback on how they are doing relative to the roles and competencies required of them (Chapter 6). Given data on their current state and information about the potential future state, they can begin to change their personal behavior to be consistent with the transformation.

Line Managers

Line managers are ultimately accountable for ensuring that the organization has the right talent and right organization in place to deliver on expectations to customers, shareholders, and communities. They have the responsibility to provide a clear business focus for the transformation, to ensure that the transformation team has access to both external and internal information, to ensure that the right people are involved in the transformation process, and to require clear and measurable results from the transformation. Numerous efforts like the war for talent, balanced scorecards, and "top company" lists have prescribed how line managers can better manage their people and organizations. The stated outcomes of the HR transformation will articulate what line managers can expect from investments in HR. A true HR transformation will reinforce the line managers' ownership and responsibility for delivering the right organization and talent to meet stakeholder needs.

The term *line manager* refers to leaders at all levels of the organization. Members of the Board of Directors should be informed about the rationale for and outcomes of the HR transformation. Discussion at the board level may elicit lessons learned and advice from companies where board members have seen similar efforts in the past and ensures that the HR transformation receives senior line management attention. Line managers in the C-suite (governing or executive committee) should be informed advisers for the transformation. A representative of this group is likely to sit on the HR transformation team. This team should be clear about how the HR transformation fits with economic, customer, and operational business goals. The team should monitor progress and help accelerate action if required. The C-suite team should assimilate lessons from the HR transformation and share them with other staff functions. They should also celebrate successes by recognizing progress and key contributors to the effort.

Line managers throughout the organization should also be aware of the HR transformation, how it will affect their ability to reach their goals, and their role in helping it move forward. The following are tips HR professionals can use as they engage line managers throughout the organization in the HR transformation:

- *Show what the transformation will mean to the bottom line and to the individual manager.* The most powerful case for transformation starts with the bottom-line impact of transformation: how change in HR focus, priorities, and delivery will increase the organization's ability to meet customer and investor expectations. The language of transformation should begin with profit and loss (see Chapter 2) and end with realistic benefits of HR transformation for profit and loss in the future. As noted earlier, without a clear and direct impact on how the company serves customers and makes or saves money, it will be difficult for an HR transformation to gain the support of executives and board members who are constantly balancing many other competing requests for time and money. Connect the HR transformation to their scorecard and accountabilities. Be sure that the financial and nonfinancial incentives of line managers are tied to the outcomes of the HR transformation. Ask them to publicly report how the HR transformation will help them with their business goals; this action will both help draw others into the process and make the managers themselves more committed to it.

- *Involve line managers as members of the transformation task force and make them part of the process.* Get them to touch it—not just watch it from the sidelines. Without their involvement, you will gain neither their commitment nor their insights. And without their engagement, you won't get their best contributions. They can be involved in defining business realities that drive the transformation (phase 1), in helping select and measure capabilities that will improve because of the transformation (phase 2), and in offering advice on how to change HR department practices and on how HR professionals should be measured and developed. They might be involved through regular interviews, updates, reviews, or participation on the transformation team. The more the key line managers are involved, the more ownership they are likely to feel.

- *Build relationships of trust by being a credible activist.* Trust grows in difficult situations. Trust develops in foxholes. When things are especially tough, building unity becomes an even more important agenda. It is at such times that it is especially important to turn to each other for support, synergy, and focus and to resolve problems in rocky relationships. Instead of going separate ways and avoiding one another, open doors and talk things through. When a line managers face critical business (or personal) problems, where do HR professionals need to find themselves? They should be in the line manager's office saying, "That must feel pretty bad. How are you feeling? What should we do to respond? What are we learning?" Let them know that you are someone they can turn to—not just with a solution, but with an open heart and mind. That is one of the greatest roles you can play in HR—to build that relationship of trust and serve as a trusted adviser. It is a powerful one, and it helps managers feel connected to what you do.

- *Be a coach who asks good questions.* Managers have to undergo public scrutiny because they are responsible for results. Sometimes they tend to retreat and become insular or isolated. One of the great levers we have in HR is to serve as coaches, on both the business and personal side of life. Sit with line managers to ask questions and listen with no personal agenda except to provide help and support. Such personal coaching is probably not going to come from finance or legal. They will more likely spend time asking the manager about money and compliance or litigation. HR is in a unique position and must ask, "How are you doing?" Ask: "Are you taking care of yourself?" As needed, recommend that the line manager get away from work to renew and reenergize.

- *Help line managers resolve common misconceptions about HR.* Help line managers overcome the common misperceptions of human resources outlined in Table 7.1 by showing how HR can deliver value to them. Often line managers have had negative experiences with an HR practice (perhaps they

Table 7.1 Common Misconceptions Held by Line Managers

MYTH	RESPONSE
Competitiveness comes from strategy.	Competitiveness = strategy × organization— and we can help you build an organization that will deliver the strategy and create competitive advantage.
Organization is structure.	Organization is capability—the things we can do because of who we are, what we value, how we work, and how we are structured.
HR professionals take care of all the people stuff so line managers don't have to spend time on it.	Much HR work is ultimately done and modeled by line managers.
HR is just common sense; anyone could do it.	HR is based on a body of researched knowledge that can be applied to achieve measurable results. HR professionals can bring that knowledge, logic, and set of competitive practices into the firm.
HR work is just a bunch of unrelated activities that have to be done.	HR work is an integrated set of outcomes that align people and organization with the strategy to achieve desired results.

weren't paid as they felt they should be, or they were kept out of a training program they felt they should attend, or they were passed over for an assignment they wanted) or with an HR professional (who may have been primarily acting as the policy police rather than as a strategic partner). By discussing myths and realities, HR professionals can begin to change the image and reputation of HR with line managers.

- *Dare to deliver the bad news to line managers.* Often HR professionals collect and distribute the results of assessments, surveys, 360-degree reviews, and other feedback or rating instruments. Frequently, the results are positive for a specific line manager, but sometimes they can be painfully negative. After delivering negative news to a key line manager, HR professionals should follow up, track progress, and encourage managers to talk about problems and to deal with them. In HR, we have to find a way to convey unwelcome news without being defensive and without creating defensiveness. Line managers are often surrounded by sycophants who share only good news. HR professionals gain credibility when they find ways to share both good news and bad and then help the line managers improve as a result of the new knowledge.

- *Stick around.* Don't just dump the HR transformation agenda on line managers. Avoid saying: "Here it is. Look at all this stuff. You go do it. I'll be back in six months." Instead, stay with them. Understand their challenges. Help them see why they need to be involved, what the outcomes will be, and how the transformation will happen. Help them understand how their lives will be better because of the HR transformation. Engage with managers, create value-added contributions, and resolve their misconceptions. They will then trust you and focus on helping HR to achieve its deliverables. Resolve the issues. Help them see what needs to happen to be successful. Listen and learn. Rather than try to change their style, work with them to use their style to produce positive results. Learn about who they are; resolve their concerns with openness and candor. If something goes wrong in HR, what do we need to do? Admit it quickly. Get it out there, and focus on the future. Create adaptability, defensibility, sociability, and stability as a way to build trust. Focus on what you deliver, not just on what you do. Keep line managers focused on the outcomes. Let them see that these deliverables are important for them.

When line managers see the value of the HR transformation for themselves and for their business, when they are involved and engaged in the HR transformation, and when they trust their HR professionals to deliver as promised, they become allies and advocates for the transformation.

TOOL 7.1	*Building an HR Transformation Team (internal):*
▶	Building the HR transformation team is critical for effective execution and long-term success. Listen to Mark Nyman describe who should be on the team from HR and line management and critical roles that must be played.
	▶ *Go to www.TransformHR.com*

External Customers and Investors

Often HR transformation comes from and is driven by an internal logic. Frequently logic, language, and practices of human resources focus on employees' needs. As an alternative, we have consistently suggested that HR transformation should focus on its impact on external stakeholders who matter to the company. We build on the basic economic principle that ultimately anything we do on the inside of a company must create value for those on the outside— or what we do is irrelevant. Organizations exist not to fulfill their own purposes but to fulfill the purposes for which society allows them to exist.

Customers, investors, and consultants can bring important external perspectives to the HR transformation process. The clear understanding of business realities so essential for real HR transformation is generally rooted in the expectations and experiences of customers and investors.

The Role of Customers in HR Transformation

The customer voice is central to a truly strategic HR transformation and may be involved in HR transformation in a number of ways. Customer information may be accessed directly via relationships HR leaders build with customers or indirectly through internal surrogates for the voice of the customer such as sales or marketing. Sales and marketing may provide the HR transformation team with customer data, experiences, and expectations that shape the desired outcomes and, therefore, the architecture of the transformation.

The results should be rooted in the firm's brand: why customers choose its products and services, what customer experience the firm hopes to provide, and what experience the customers are actually having with the firm—and how it can be improved. When HR practices are redesigned, they should align to ensure consistency with customer expectations. Customers can also be directly and actively involved in HR transformation, for example, by having HR professionals visit them to find out what organizational capabilities and leadership competencies they expect from the company. Many companies expect their HR professionals to spend time regularly (for example, one day a quarter) with external customers to stay in touch with customer needs and trends and better understand how HR practices impact company performance in meeting customer expectations. The line of sight between HR transformation and customer share (revenue from targeted or key customers) should be clear, understood, and shared. The following three steps can help link external customers and HR transformation.

Step 1: Collect Customer Insights and Information

When seeking to transform HR based on the voice of the customer, HR professionals must have information and insights about the customers. The first insight focuses on who the customers are. At P&G, for example, the customers are both the consumers who use the products and the retailers who sell them. For BNP Paribas, customers range from checking account holders to commercial finance brokers. At Cardinal Heath, they are hospital administrators, physicians, patients, and insurance companies. The second insight that HR professionals must understand is the customers' buying criteria: why they buy from one source and not from another. To access these insights, HR professionals can regularly review the business environment their customers are working in, the threats they face, and the opportunities they seek to capitalize on (see Chapter 2). They can synthesize data about customer financial conditions, and about consumer expectations and spending trends. HR professionals should know the customer as well as the salespeople do, because while sales offers product or solutions to a customer, HR establishes the individual talent and organizational capabilities that create products, services, and relationships that meet customers' long-term expectations. In so doing, HR offers a relationship with the customer that goes beyond any single transaction.

Step 2: Recognize Moments of Truth and Touch Points

Along with all employees in an organization, HR professionals must understand the business's moments of truth or critical touch points. P&G identified two key moments of truth: one when the consumer picks the P&G product from the shelf in a store, and the other when the consumer uses and develops an opinion about the product. Each company must identify the moments of truth for its customers. HR professionals should also recognize these moments, knowing and understanding what causes them and how they tie to the financial success of the firm. HR professionals who regularly reinforce the moments of truth make sure that their HR actions are guided by customer expectations.

Step 3: Sustain Customer Experience with HR Practices

HR can play a key role in managing and evaluating the customer experience. Working with sales, marketing, quality, and other functions, HR can support focus groups, customer service evaluations, and other data-gathering activities. HR should also be a key player in data analysis and synthesis.

HR professionals are in a unique position to deliver on the promises salespeople make by ensuring that the organization is able to execute them successfully. Sales tends to deliver a single event ("We will provide you the product or service you contracted for"); HR can complement this event by making it into a pattern ("We will build an organization that continually meets your needs"). Using customer information they have gathered, HR leaders must make changes in staffing, training, communication, rewards and recognition, organizational structure, and leadership that sustain a customer connection. Knowing the customers and understanding why, where, and when they buy the product will greatly enhance HR's ability to make decisions in systems, practice, and policy design that will improve the customer experience. Our case study companies agree that HR systems, practices, and policies must be clearly aligned with customers. They also say that their experience has shown that leadership and rewards are the two areas that can have the most impact on improving customer experience, and therefore increasing revenue.

Once the three steps of the customer connection model are taken, a system must be established to sustain long-term customer connectivity. HR leaders need to create sustainable processes that ensure that the customer is either present or represented in the room when programs and practices are designed for people, performance, information, and work. An effective example of this is Hallstein Moerk, chief HR officer at Nokia. When Moerk gathered his senior HR team at the end of 2007 to plan the major HR strategy and initiatives for 2008, he invited two customers to participate in the meeting. Every time the HR team came up with a new program or initiative, the team would ask the customers to weigh in. Sometimes the customers would say, "Yes, that's exactly what we need," yet other times they would say, "Sounds like an interesting idea, but it doesn't help me!" Customers in the room proved to be a significant benefit for Moerk and his Nokia team. When there is a clear line of sight between HR investments and customer requirements, both customers and HR win.

HR leaders can also broker opportunities for their professionals to have regular face-to-face interaction with customers. As a function, HR has core capabilities that can and ought to be used to deliver value for customers. For example, several HR departments partner with customers to provide training, develop leadership, and do team building. Royal Bank of Scotland requires its HR team to spend at least two days each year interacting with customers (in a call center, at a branch, or in some other environment).

Regular face-to-face time between human resources and customers is beneficial for both parties. For true long-term sustainability, however, HR must take these partnering relationships a step further and be a regular and active participant in the sales process. A salesperson who engages with a customer can promote a successful interaction (for example, "Buy my product or service and it will solve your problem today"). However, when an HR person participates in the sale, the company can promise the customer a future pattern rather than simply a one-time event. Instead of just buying a product or service, customers can be clear about buying a relationship because they know that HR has the ability to ensure that talent and organizational systems are in place to guarantee long-term delivery. In this new paradigm, HR in the customers' mind becomes the creator and guardian of the long-term relationship. This is the future of HR; a salesperson would be remiss to attempt to sell a product or service as an event without involving HR, which can sell the longer-term relationship.

The Role of Investors in HR Transformation

Like customers, investors should influence and be influenced by HR transformation. When an HR transformation is effective, investors have more confidence in future earnings because the capabilities that result from the transformation should help ensure sustainable business success. Research shows that economic intangibles such as organizational capabilities represent up to 50 percent of the market value of a firm. In good and bad economic conditions, companies with a higher-quality organization (leadership, HR practices, culture, and governance) will be likely to have higher P/E ratios than their competitors. HR can bring the logic and values of investors into the HR transformation work. Investors factor into the HR transformation as HR departments align their practices with the requirements of the investment community. Investors' logic and values may be accessed when the HR transformation team invites key investors into their deliberations. By so doing, the HR team not only accesses investor logic but also communicates to the involved investors that their values are being inculcated into the company's institutional infrastructure. Investor confidence will then positively influence the investors' buy-or-sell decisions. The same steps for customers apply to investors:

Step 1: Collect Investor Insights and Information
HR professionals should know whom their firm targets as its key investors and why they invest. For publicly traded firms, this generally means major investors and analysts who follow their industry. For divisions of large companies, the investor is the corporate headquarters, which allocates money across

divisions. For privately held companies, the investor may be the family or other owner. For public agencies, the investors may be legislators who make policies and who allocate resources to support some agencies more than others. In any case, HR professionals should know who the relevant investors are and how they evaluate your organization's success.

Step 2: Recognize Investor Moments of Truth

HR professionals should be aware of investor contact points. This might include regular investor phone calls, meetings, or data. HR professionals can help deliver value by making sure these investor encounters convey the information about organizational capabilities discussed in Chapter 3. A good example of this was a large telecommunications company that regularly invited investors to its senior executive development programs. During these programs, company leaders were continually reminded of the investors' expectations, and the investors came to understand the company's direction and the abilities of its future leaders. With this information, investors gained confidence in the company's future earnings capability.

Step 3: Sustain Investor Confidence with HR Practices

As you design your HR practices with regard to people, performance, information, and work, make sure they pass an investor filter. Are each of the practices designed and delivered to increase investor awareness and confidence and meet investors' expectations? Does HR actively participate in understanding investors who have both positive and negative perceptions of the company? Does HR help ensure that investors know and understand your organization's success in creating and sustaining key capabilities (especially as measured against your competitors)?

Consultants and Advisers

A colleague with deep expertise in M&A integration recently shared that he had been retained to help a client manage a merger integration. But the client, in an effort to cut costs, opted to not use these services and worked to integrate the merger without outside advice. Six months later, the client had not realized the synergies it had promised the investment community when it made the merger. Key employees had left, the combined company strategy was haphazard, and leaders were questioning whether they had made the right choice in the merger. We cannot guarantee that our colleague could have averted these problems, but we know that he had experience in dozens of companies who had faced and overcome these and other problems.

We recommend the judicious and targeted use of outside consultants as partners in advancing the HR transformation. As consultants and educators, we have seen clients who employ the services of consultants effectively and also those who do not. Here are some hints in retaining consultants for the HR transformation:

- *Contract clearly and specifically for the outcomes of the engagement.* What input will the consultant bring? What processes will be used? Who will the consultant place as on-site personnel?
- *Verify that your consultants are educated in the key business challenges that confront your company.* Provide the consultants with information about customer trends, investor perceptions, targeted capabilities, leadership bench strength, and employee competencies. Occasionally and tactfully quiz your consultants about the extent to which they have grasped and are using that information in their work with you.
- *Confirm that the consultant has a clear, proven point of view with expertise in the content.* Many generalist firms offer generic models and project management support, but unless your goal is simply to hire extra hands, be clear about the content expertise your consultant brings.
- *Make sure the consulting firm will adapt its ideas, not require you to adopt them verbatim.* Adaptation means that the consultant is willing to modify some of the key principles based on your unique situation. Adoption means that the consultant wants you to use its off-the-shelf ideas as they stand.
- *Transfer knowledge to your team.* External knowledge should be leased to own, not rented. This means having the consultants not only share their

models, frameworks, and experiences but transfer their insights to key people in your organization.

- *Make sure that the consultants offer a holistic view of HR transformation.* Be wary of a firm that proposes a piecemeal approach, changing only one element of the larger transformation we have proposed.

Our experience suggests that consultants can add value in a number of specific ways and at a number of specific points in the process:

Assessing the Need for Transformation

- Spend a day with consultants, talking about how their most successful client companies have approached transformation.
- Engage them to assist in designing the assessment process and training internal staff to conduct the assessment.
- Involve them in providing access to other HR leaders and sharing their experiences on transformation and what is involved.

Setting Goals

- Use consultants to facilitate the goal-setting process for transformation.
- Involve them in providing insight into ways other companies have gone about setting goals for transformation; essentially, ask them to help you test whether your transformation plans are ambitious enough or too ambitious.
- Invite them to test the goals for potential problems that may not be anticipated.

Planning for Implementation

- Invite the consultants to identify potential obstacles and potholes they have seen hinder the transformation efforts of other companies.
- Discuss ways of gaining stakeholder involvement and support.
- Ask the consultants to help develop the implementation plan and time table.
- Involve the consultants in facilitating the change process.

Evaluating the Effectiveness of Transformation

- Engage the consultants to assist, facilitate, or lead the evaluation process and to provide an objective point of reference.

In short, external consultants often add value by bringing in experiences from other companies, by previewing and averting common challenges, by not being beholden to a political system that might limit creative problem solving, and by being independent contributors to the HR transformation process. As in any decision to use a consultant, success depends on the choice of the right consultant involved in the right way at the right time.

Combining Different Viewpoints into an HR Transformation Team

An HR transformation team should include representatives of the four groups we define in this chapter: HR leaders, line managers, customers and investors, and consultants. It should be sponsored by the CHRO, who should accept accountability for the design and delivery of the HR transformation. It is often chaired by the head of HR for HR and staffed with HR representatives from business units and centers of expertise, line managers from a mix of businesses including a member of the C-suite, an outside adviser, and representatives of customers and investors. This team meets regularly to set and deliver on milestones of the HR transformation (discussed in Chapter 8).

TOOL 7.2	*Building an HR Transformation Team (external)*
	Now that you've decided who from HR and line management should be on your HR transformation team, how are you going to involve customers, investors, and external thought leaders? Listen to Jon Younger describe essential external roles for HR transformation.
	▶ *Go to www.TransformHR.com*

CHAPTER 8

MAKING IT HAPPEN

8

Even with a careful description of the phases and details of doing an HR transformation, change is hard. Transforming the HR department is far more difficult than people generally anticipate. Making change happen involves two challenges: identifying in a logical way what should happen (this is the *content* of the transformation), and turning that content into what actually happens (this is the *process* of the transformation). We discuss each in this chapter as a blueprint for making HR transformation happen.

What Should Happen: Milestones, Activities, and Outcomes

In any transformation, the pieces come together in milestones, activities, and outcomes. Milestones represent *what* should be done; activities define *how* it is done; and outcomes monitor *how to tell* if it has been done well. As we have worked with many companies who have succeeded (and faltered) in HR transformation, we have identified a set of 13 milestones, activities, and outcomes that turn the four phases into an action plan.

The milestones are presented in a linear way, but they are unlikely to happen strictly sequentially. The timing of the transformation may vary according to your culture, the changes you anticipate making, the resistance you expect to encounter, and the level of support you have from the broader organization. But when you understand and adapt the 13 milestones, you will be more successful in your transformation. It may be tempting to skip some of the milestones, but if you do, you will probably have to backtrack and consider the missing milestones in order to make progress.

Phase 1: Business Context

Milestone 1: Formally acknowledge that an HR transformation initiative would be of value.

- *Activity:* The CHRO determines that the timing is right for an HR transformation by affirming that business conditions are conducive to it, that HR could offer more value to the company, and that senior line leaders would be supportive of the effort. This determination is likely to come from observations about the business and from conversations with other business leaders.
- *Outcome:* CHRO becomes a sponsor and initial champion of the HR transformation. Line managers understand the rationale and benefit for the transformation and how it will respond to business conditions and are at least initially supportive.
- *Tools:* 2.1 HR Transformation Readiness Assessment
    2.2 Preparing for HR Transformation Video
    2.3 HR Transformation Jumpstart Methods

Milestone 2: Create a transformation team.
- *Activity:* The CHRO forms, with the support of the senior leaders of the organization, an HR transformation team. This team should include a broad spectrum of HR leaders and professionals (including those from centers of expertise and embedded HR) as well as representatives from line management. The team should also be attuned to the voice of the customer and investor either directly (by having customers and investors involved) or indirectly (by collecting and applying pertinent customer and investor data as a team). This team should form a clear charter about how it will approach transformation, including the four phases that we propose. The team should also define its governance practices: how often it will meet, what decisions it will make, how it will make those decisions, what budget it will require, and so on.
- *Outcome:* An HR transformation team is formed with a clear charter for promoting the HR transformation. The team is sponsored by line managers and recognized throughout the organization as credible and viable.

- *Tools:* 7.1 Building an HR Transformation Team (internal)

  7.2 Building an HR Transformation Team (external)

Milestone 3: Define, assess, and prioritize the new business realities that require HR transformation and change.

- *Activity:* Under the direction of the HR transformation team, an assessment is made of the business realities facing the organization (see Chapter 2). Information about these business realities may come from interviews with managers and staff specialists inside the company, from interviews with industry leaders (investors, analysts, trade association members, and other thought leaders) outside the company, and from business data (such as reports of technology trends in the industry). The HR implications of these business realities are identified and shared with the senior business team and with HR professionals throughout the organization.

- *Outcome:* A clear statement of business realities is articulated that helps people know why the transformation is occurring and how key stakeholders will benefit from the effort.

- *Tools:* 2.4 Stakeholder Analysis Worksheet

  2.5 External Environment Video

Milestone 4: Complete and communicate the business case for doing HR transformation.

- *Activity:* The HR transformation team prepares a business case for transformation, defining what an HR transformation is, explaining why the transformation should happen, and laying out a road map for doing the transformation. This HR transformation proposal can be presented to the Board of Directors, senior executive team, HR leadership team, and HR professionals throughout the organization. It can also be included in presentations by senior leaders as they discuss how they will respond to business strategies going forward.

- *Outcome:* Key participants in the HR transformation (business leaders, HR professionals, and employees) understand why HR transformation is a timely activity.
- *Tools:* 2.6 Business Case Worksheet
  2.7 HR Transformation Business Case Video

Phase 2: Outcomes

Milestone 5: Do an organizational capabilities audit to identity the top two to four capabilities required by the business strategy.

- *Activity:* For the organizational unit where the HR transformation is occurring (corporate, business unit, division, country, or plant), perform an organizational capabilities audit. Prepare a list of possible capabilities and phrase them in terms relevant to your business. Ask a cross-section of individuals to assess the relative importance of these capabilities given the business strategy. Prioritize the most important capabilities for the organization. Make these capabilities the outcomes of the transformation. Share this information with key stakeholders of the transformation.
- *Outcome:* The organizational capabilities are identified and shared.
- *Tools:* 3.1 Organizational Capabilities Video
  3.2 Organizational Capability Assessment

Milestone 6: Operationalize the key capabilities and state them as the outcomes of the HR transformation.

- *Activity:* Turn the capabilities identified at Milestone 5 (in the capability audit) into specific measures that can be monitored and tracked. These measures can be created by brainstorming what indicators will show whether these capabilities are accomplished. These indicators can then be put into behavior- and results-based measures. These measures should be validated and aligned with the balanced scorecard for the organization and with the accountabilities for line managers.

- *Outcome:* The deliverables of the transformation are turned into a scorecard. Everyone knows what the results of the transformation should be.
- *Tools:* 3.3 Operationalizing Your Capabilities Video

Milestone 7: Show how accomplishment of these capabilities will benefit employees, line managers, customers, investors, communities, and other stakeholders.

- *Activity:* Each of the key stakeholders who would be affected by the HR transformation is identified. The outcome of the HR transformation for each stakeholder should be defined in specific, measurable outcomes. This milestone can occur by having a subgroup of the HR transformation team gather information about the current and potential relationship of each stakeholder to the organization. This information is revealed by answers to the question, If this HR transformation is successful, what will [listed stakeholder] receive? The answers can come from interviews with stakeholders or those who work directly with those stakeholders.
- *Outcome:* An HR transformation stakeholder map can be prepared that shows the value of the HR transformation for each stakeholder.
- *Tools:* 3.4 Mapping Capabilities to Stakeholders

Phase 3: HR Redesign

Milestone 8: Create an HR strategy statement: who we are, what we do, and why we do it.

- *Activity:* Work with your senior HR team, involving other key stakeholders, to build an HR strategy statement (this has been called an HR vision, mission, purpose, or other statement). As we suggest in Chapter 4, this statement should answer these questions:
  1. Who are we? (Your statement of your identity and reputation as an HR department.)
  2. What do we deliver? (Your summary of the work that you perform as an HR department.)

3. Why do we do it? (Your definition of the outcomes of your HR work with focus on the key capabilities that are required for business success.)

This HR strategy statement should be discussed and validated with line managers, the HR community, and others in the organization. It should align with the process of the HR transformation. It should be discussed and referred to regularly in HR meetings and forums. It should be a guide for hiring new people into HR, promoting people into senior positions within HR, and developing future HR professionals.

- *Outcome:* Those inside and outside the HR community will understand the strategy of the HR department.
- *Tools:* 4.1 HR Strategy Statement Worksheet
        4.2 Drafting a Powerful HR Strategy Video

Milestone 9: Shape the HR organization with clear accountabilities for centers of expertise, embedded HR, operational HR, shared services, and corporate.

- *Activity:* Create a clear focus on strategic work and transactional work. The way your HR department is organized assigns accountabilities and shapes how HR work is done. As discussed in Chapter 4, there are five general areas of responsibility or channels in which HR professionals might work:

Service Centers

Corporate HR (HR Oversight)

Embedded HR (Strategic Business Partnering)

Centers of Expertise (HR Expertise)

Operational Execution

Your HR transformation team can define the expectations of each of these five areas as appropriate. The team will then audit the extent to which each of the five areas might apply in your company. Some companies have clear distinctions among the five areas. Others combine some of these areas of work because of the scale or focus of their department. The key consideration is to ensure that the structure of the HR organization is consistent with the structure of the business organization. As the structure of the HR department is clarified, you can begin to identify key positions within these five channels. The requirements or job description for each work area can be delineated and people can be matched to those positions. Ensuring that roles are focused on either strategic or transactional work will increase the effectiveness and efficiency of both.

Implementation of the HR structure often begins by investing in technology to make sure that HR shared services can deliver the administrative duties of HR. The responsibilities of corporate, centers of expertise, embedded HR, and operational HR are then defined and staffed. It is also important to create a charter of how the different groups will work with each other: what information will they share, how will they make decisions, and so on. A new HR structure often requires not only the right organization chart, with work areas, positions, and people filled in, it also requires an agreed-upon process to come to these decisions. Ideally, those who are named on the organization chart are given the opportunity to participate in defining their respective roles and responsibilities.

It can also be useful to create what we call a "rules of engagement" charter. The rules of engagement charter clarifies how those in each of the HR work areas connect with each other in terms of information sharing, decision making, activity support, and required resources. This charter can also specify how employees and line managers can access the HR department to meet their needs.

- *Outcome:* The HR department has an organization chart with positions and reporting relationships defined and a charter for how the HR department will work together to meet needs of its stakeholders.
- *Tools:* 4.3 Strategic vs. Transactional Work Video

Milestone 10: Audit HR practices to prioritize those that will align with strategy, integrate with each other, and be innovative.

- *Activity*: Auditing HR practices helps prioritize where to invest money, time, and people to deliver the most value. Here are several different ways to audit HR practices:

  1. *Best practices*. You can define the best practices for people, performance, information, and work, then measure the extent to which your company performs against these standards. If you are sure you know what the best practices are, this approach provides valuable information regarding the extent to which your organization delivers against these new standards.

  2. *Perceptions*. You can do an HR 360-degree audit where employees, line managers, and HR professionals assess the extent to which they perceive HR practices as delivering value to them and to your organization. This approach, which we call "Beauty is in the eye of the beholder," helps you discover the perceived value of the HR practices to those who are using them.

  3. *Strategy*. You can measure the extent to which each HR practice aligns with your organization's strategy. You do this by scoring the extent to which each HR practice facilitates the creation of organizational capabilities and the accomplishment of your business strategy. This assessment helps you know which HR practices are helping accomplish strategy.

  4. *Integration*. You can measure the extent to which your HR practices connect with each other through an integration audit. To do this audit, create a matrix with HR practices listed on both axes, then in each cell note the extent to which the practices coincide with each other. For example, if you are hiring new employees on skills ABC, and training employees to master skills ABC, you have a +10 connection, but if you are hiring employees based on skills ABC, but training DEF, you have a -10 connection. This assessment helps you determine the extent to which your HR practices work together.

  If you are most worried about how up-to-date and forward-looking your HR practices are, we recommend the best practices audit to compare your thinking to that of world-class organizations in your field and in others; if you are most worried about the reputation of your HR department, audit perceptions; if you are most worried about how HR impacts the business, choose strategy; and if you are most worried about offering an integrated approach in HR, choose the integration audit. Leading companies often use multiple approaches to HR audits so that they can create a full picture of the quality of their HR investments.

Regardless of the HR audit you use, your goal is to prioritize which HR practices should receive a disproportionate investment of money, time, and talent. Investing equally in all HR practices may make you good at many, but not excellent in any. In prioritizing, it is helpful to identify which HR practices may lead to effectiveness in other practices.

- *Outcome:* You will be able to clearly articulate which HR practices you should invest in to deliver value. This creates a blueprint for where to prioritize HR work.
- *Tools:* 5.1 The Six Bs Overview

    5.2 VOI^{2}C^{2}E Overview

    5.3 Strategy Assessment Worksheet

    5.4 Transforming HR Practices Video

Milestone 11: Define what makes an effective HR professional in terms of role, competencies, and activities.

- *Activity:* Upgrading your HR professionals will ultimately determine the success of your transformation. Under the direction of the HR transformation team, you might form a project team charged to create a competency model for HR professionals. They begin this effort by specifying what your HR professionals must know and do to be successful. The definition of success comes as you consider roles and activities for HR, but culminates in being clear about competencies HR professionals must demonstrate to be effective. You can create standards for HR professionals by building on research about what makes an effective HR professional (see our work on *HR Competencies*), then adapting that research to your organization. This adaptation comes from interviewing business leaders, customers, investors, and HR leaders to find out what they expect more and less of from HR professionals in your organization.

- *Outcome:* You will have a standard for what makes an HR professional effective that results in a competency model for HR professionals.
- *Tools:* 6.1 HR Competencies Overview

  6.2 HR Competencies Research Summary

  6.3 HR Competencies Assessments

Milestone 12: Assess and invest in HR professionals to make sure they have the abilities to deliver on the transformation.

- *Activity:* Using your organization's HR competency model, you can assess your HR professionals on the extent to which they do or do not demonstrate these competencies. Doing 360-degree reviews for HR helps all your HR professionals assess their strengths and weaknesses. Each HR professional can receive a personal report to use as the basis for an individual improvement plan. This improvement plan focuses on how the HR professional can upgrade skills through training, job experience, and personal learning. Investing in HR development helps your HR professionals meet higher expectations.
- *Outcome:* HR professionals will all know what is expected to be effective on the job, will learn how well they measure up against those expectations, and will be able to prepare a personal development plan for how to improve.
- *Tools:* 6.4 Strategic HR Professional Development Video

Phase 4: HR Accountability

Milestone 13: Make sure that the transformation team is staffed by the right mix of people and engaged in the right activities.

- *Activity:* At the beginning of your HR transformation, you form a transformation team to direct and oversee the transformation. This team has an ongoing responsibility to make sure that the transformation proceeds in a timely and coherent way. They should develop a blueprint for the overall transformation that puts into a responsibility chart the milestones we have presented. This blueprint should be regularly reviewed and updated to keep the transformation on track. The transformation team also contracts for the organizational capability audit and the HR audits of departments, practices, or people. The team evaluates these data and creates streams of work that move the transformation forward. The team continually communicates progress and the next steps of the transformation to key stakeholders. The team tracks results of the transformation to declare success and identify areas of improvement.

- *Outcome:* A high-performing HR transformation team will make sure that the transformation makes progress. You know if your HR transformation team is doing well if the transformation stays on track and delivers the results declared in Phase 2.
- *Tools:* 8.1 HR Transformation Milestones Checklist

    8.2 Pilot's Checklist

    8.3 Accountability and Change Video

TOOL 8.1	*HR Transformation Milestones Checklist*
	Use the HR Transformation Milestones Checklist as a guide throughout your transformation process. Download a printable copy of the Milestones Checklist.
	▶ *Go to www.TransformHR.com*

Turning What Should Happen into What Does Happen

The logical milestones are a blueprint for how to proceed with your HR transformation. Now it becomes important to make the blueprint come to life. In our work on managing change within organizations, we have found that sometimes good blueprints are not implemented as intended. A major challenge of any change effort is to turn what clearly should be done (the milestones for HR transformation) into what is actually done. For the last 20 years, we have studied effective organization change and found the seven key factors shown in Table 8.1, each of which helps turn good intentions into successful reality. You can adapt these seven conditions for success to help make your HR transformation happen.

You can audit these seven conditions for success at the beginning, middle, and end of your transformation project. This change profile points you

Table 8.1 *Conditions for Successful Change*

CONDITIONS FOR SUCCESSFUL CHANGE	IMPLICATIONS FOR HR TRANSFORMATION
Leading: Having leadership support for the change	Gaining leadership support for the HR transformation: line and HR
Creating a shared need: Knowing why you are doing the transformation	Building a case for why HR transformation adds value
Envisioning: Developing a clear sense of the outcomes of the transformation	Having a model of what HR transformation includes: practices, functions, people
Engaging: Mobilizing commitment from key individuals	Getting buy-in from everyone, line and HR (steering committee)
Decision making: Knowing the decisions that need to be made to move the transformation forward	Starting small by focusing on early decisions
Institutionalizing: Making sure that the transformation integrates with business activities	Weaving the HR transformation into all HR practices and resource allocation systems in the company
Monitoring and learning: Tracking the success of the transformation	Refining and adjusting the blueprint, tracking progress, and learning from the transformation

to where you need to focus to help your transformation make progress. For example, when the HR transformation team is formed, it might do a change profile to plot where it needs to dedicate more time and attention. This change audit responds to seven diagnostic questions, each rated on a 0–10 scale:

To what extent does your HR transformation have . . .

1. *A leader:* Public and legitimate leadership inside and outside HR to champion the HR transformation?
2. *A shared need:* A line of sight to new business realities to show how HR will deliver value to those realities?
3. *A vision:* Clearly defined outcomes and results of the HR transformation?
4. *Engagement:* Support from the individuals who will have to implement it?
5. *Decisions:* A list of the decisions that need to be made in HR departments, about practices, and by people to make the transformation happen?
6. *Institutionalization:* Sufficient institutional support to make sure that it goes forward (budget, people, information, technology) and is integrated with other business processes?
7. *Measurement:* Metrics in place to monitor how you are doing and how you can improve?

The answers to these questions can be profiled on a chart like the one in Figure 8.1 to diagnose where you need to focus to make the most progress on your transformation. The following sections offer suggestions for creating each of these seven conditions for success.

TOOL 8.2	*Pilot's Checklist*
	Download a printable copy of the Pilot's Checklist and learn more about resources for sustainable change management.
	▶ *Go to www.TransformHR.com*

Figure 8.1 *Profile of HR Transformation*

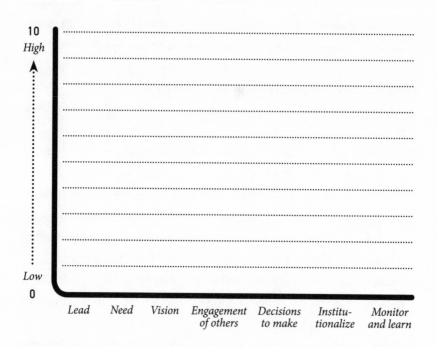

Leading Change

Leaders of any change sponsor, champion, and model the change. They sponsor the change by making it a priority, by allocating resources (money and people) to it, and by tracking it to make sure it is on target. The sponsors of the HR transformation will probably be the CHRO and members of the executive team who see HR transformation as critical to business success. A champion is the leader of the transformation who has primary accountability for moving it forward, dedicates a sizable portion of time to it, and governs its day-to-day activities. In large companies, this individual is often the person charged with HR for HR or another person who is assigned to chair the daily work of the HR transformation team. All leaders involved need to personally model a commitment to change. For HR transformation, this means that leaders inside and outside HR need to encourage innovative ideas, to be open to changing their behavior, and to be willing to make investments to make HR transformation succeed.

Creating a Shared Need

Change does not happen until the need for change is greater than the resistance to change. Almost any change is uncomfortable, requiring growth, learning, and experimenting with new behaviors. When we engage in any personal change, we risk embarrassment and failure. Most of us are unwilling to change without a clear and compelling reason. For HR transformation, the imperative for change comes from dissatisfaction with some element in the present, or a compelling vision of what could be, or both.

The HR transformation team should maintain both dissatisfaction with HR's present situation and a compelling vision of a better future for HR's contribution. Dissatisfaction with the status quo can generally be promoted by asking questions like these:

- *What are our HR stakeholders telling us?* Find and use quotes from employees, line managers, customers, or investors to illustrate problems that need to be addressed. Broadly communicate examples of HR failures and their impact on the organization.
- *How are we performing relative to other HR functions?* Compare data from competency surveys or department audits with other companies or other business units in your organization. Use benchmark data such as headcount ratios or revenue percentages.
- *What do we do that is in conflict with our stated or implicit organizational, individual, and functional goals and values?* Do we say HR helps line managers change and resist changing ourselves? Do we talk about high performance without standards or consequences?

The trick to maintaining productive dissonance, however, is not in identifying every area of failure or unmet expectations. It is in choosing the examples that support the most pressing areas of improvement and then using that information to maintain an imperative for change that fluctuates in response to the HR organization's resources for changing.

Shaping a Vision

It is too easy and too common for the transformation team to focus only on HR structure (who reports to whom, who influences what, or how to build an organization chart) and HR practices (ways of dealing with talent, training, compensation, and other matters). It is important for the transformation team to pay attention to the outcomes of Phase 1 (why do transformation) and Phase 2 (outcomes of the transformation). These reinforce the vision or purpose of the transformation. When these outcomes are continually emphasized, the required details of changing HR organization, practices, and people can continue to be successfully rooted in fundamental purposes. When the inevitable debates occur about what should be done to further the transformation, a return to these basic purposes will generally provide direction. For example, one company was bogged down in determining the balance of power between embedded HR professionals and centers of expertise. Each group lobbied for a more central role in delivering HR value. As a result, they spent more time choosing sides than making progress. To resolve this debate, the transformation team returned to the business conditions, which highlighted mature markets, aging products, and the importance of building innovation as a primary corporate capability. By revisiting these key strategic considerations, they were able to focus on where HR could foster the most innovation, either at the corporate level or in the businesses. This led them to successfully forge a consensus about how to resolve the debate.

A test of the vision of the HR transformation is to ask multiple stakeholders—from C-suite executives to the HR executive team to employees to HR professionals throughout the organization—a simple question: If the HR transformation is successful, what will happen? Gaining consensus on this question confirms the vision of the transformation.

Engaging Others

In any change effort, about 20 percent of employees are supportive and willing to change; 20 percent are laggards who will resist and are unlikely to change no matter what the sponsor does, and 60 percent can be convinced to change. It is seductive to surround yourself with those who are already committed to a change effort or to spend time and energy trying to convert the laggards, but neither approach works. Instead, conserve your energy, building on the supporters and working around the resisters, and focus on the middle 60 percent. People become engaged when they fully participate in the change effort. This participation comes from sharing information, behaving as if already committed, and reinforcing the new required behaviors.

In HR transformation, it is important to recognize the stakeholders who will be affected by the transformation, including line managers, HR leaders at the top of the HR organization, HR staff throughout the organization, and other employees. Involving representatives of these groups can be done directly as they participate in transformation discussions and decisions. It can also be done indirectly, by making sure that their concerns and ideas are represented in discussions. By involving key stakeholders, either in presence or in essence, you can help increase their engagement with the process.

Making Decisions

For the HR transformation to be effective, a series of decisions need to be made. We have found that most good leaders are willing to make decisions when the decision protocol is clear. We have found five rules that form a decision protocol and help move any change effort forward (see Table 8.2). These five rules can be applied by the transformation team to make progress in a disciplined way.

Table 8.2 Decision Rules and HR Transformation

DECISION AREA	RULE	APPLICATION FOR HR TRANSFORMATION
Decision clarity	Ensure clarity about what decisions need to be made.	The HR transformation team should identify choices for each of the following decisions: • HR transformation team: Membership and leadership • HR case for change: Who makes the case and who prepares the summary • HR transformation outcomes: What they are and how to recognize them • HR department: Reporting relationships • HR practices: Which ones to prioritize and how to change them • HR professionals: How to upgrade their skills and knowledge
Decision responsibility	Assign someone to be responsible for making the decision.	• Someone should be responsible for each of the key decisions. The responsible person might be the CHRO, head of HR for HR, or someone else who is assigned that task.
Decision time-line	Make sure that there is a public deadline for when the decision will be made.	• The deadline for each decision can be established depending on the scope and scale of the decision. The more public the deadline, the better.
Decision process	Create a process to make the decision (right people, right rigor, and so forth).	• The decision process defines how the decision is made: Who is involved in the decision (from HR, line, and external stakeholders), how accurate the decision should be (the risk the HR choice implies), and first steps for making the decision
Decision follow-up	Track and monitor the decision to follow up.	• Tracking implies measurement and knowing if the decision is accurate so that learning and improvement can occur.

When these rules are applied to the decisions the HR transformation team must make, the team is more likely to make them in a timely way.

Institutionalizing

Institutionalizing HR transformation requires embedding the transformation into the organization so that it lasts over time by integrating the HR work streams and building it into the culture.

Integrating HR Work

While this book examines HR department structures, HR practices, and HR people in separate chapters, treating the three as separate issues during the transformation effort will result in misalignments that will make it impossible to achieve the desired outcomes. In real life, department structures, practices, and people should be addressed in parallel, not in sequence. For example, if you tinker with the performance management system to create greater collaboration, you are going to have to ensure that training programs also promote greater collaboration. Managing the integration among changes to people, practices, and departments will likely take a lot of time and directed effort early in the transformation. Over time, happily, the integrated processes tend to become standardized and routine. The HR transformation team has to look at the current state of the overall HR department through the lens of the initiative's desired outcomes and identify what should be changed and how—and then ensure that HR processes, structures, and people are integrated and aligned.

Changing the Culture

Our definition of *culture* is the pattern of activities inside a company that reflect external customer and investor expectations. In practice, it is easy to focus on events and activities, not patterns. To create lasting change, however, it is essential to focus less on the event or activity and more on the series of activities (the pattern). In your HR transformation, address the initiative not as a one-time event or even a series of related events but as a new pattern of behavior that is the embodiment of a new pattern of thinking. Creating new patterns happens when the activities involved are assimilated into the way work is done. Change is not something that happens in a workshop, team meeting, or process review; it occurs naturally and continuously during all work activities. Creating a new mind-set means that HR leaders model and encourage HR professionals to constantly learn, unlearn, improve, and accept the inevitability of change.

A new pattern means that a new culture is created. We have found that cultures endure when the culture inside focuses on customers outside. The changes HR employees and organizations make inside can and should be clearly and directly linked to the expectations of customers and investors. Change is not an idle hazing meant to distract employees; it is a means of improving all aspects of the company direction and results. Events turn into patterns and actions become assimilated. Identity is formed and change lasts.

Monitoring and Learning

Any transformation requires measurement of progress that enables you to see what is and what is not working. From such measurements, learning occurs and improvements can be made. HR leaders need to identify and measure leading indicators so they can identify early signs of success or failure and implement learning mechanisms that will allow the function to identify what worked well and what didn't, investigate why, and create changes to ensure improved future performance. Learning becomes a virtuous cycle when tracking relevant indicators leads to insight, which leads to continuous improvement and future learning, which lead to better results that can then be measured. In successful organizations, monitoring and learning occur continuously, in both good and bad times.

Leaders committed to continuous monitoring gather information about what worked and what did not, track both quantitative and qualitative data from multiple sources, and identify trends and themes from the data. They measure what is right to measure—not just what is easy—by tracking behaviors (what was done) as leading indicators and outcomes (what was accomplished) as lag indicators. Leaders who learn see patterns in events, think critically and creatively about problems, are candid and self-aware about strengths and weaknesses, try new things, adapt best practices, and continuously seek feedback.

Institutionalizing also means that the new HR direction and aspirations are embedded in HR systems. This means that new HR professionals are hired who have skills for future expectations and that HR training, performance management, compensation, and communication are designed and delivered so as to create the organizational capabilities that are the key outcomes of the transformation. As this happens, the HR transformation will begin to have sustained successes that can be celebrated both inside and outside the HR department, appreciating successes and learning from failures.

Summary: The Process for Doing HR Transformation

When these seven conditions exist, the milestones for the HR transformation are much more likely to be accomplished. As these milestones occur, HR professionals become full partners in helping a business move forward. HR can help organizations get the maximum value from their people and their organization while ensuring they treat them as individuals with unique needs, aspirations, and dreams. What a privilege to be able to be HR professionals who can achieve goals that improve both the world of business and the world of people!

TOOL 8.3	*Accountability and Change*
▶	You've read the book; now it's time to make change happen. Listen to Dave Ulrich's closing remarks and charge to the HR profession.
	▶ *Go to www.TransformHR.com*

II

TALES FROM THE TRENCHES: TRANSFORMATION CASE STUDIES

CASE STUDY OVERVIEW

If a picture paints a thousand words, we hope that, conversely, our "thousand words" in the following pages will adequately paint a picture of real HR transformation in real companies, carried out by real people. In this section, we present cases from RBL Institute members Flextronics, Pfizer, Intel, and Takeda, who each graciously accepted our invitation to share their stories of HR transformation. We must note here that true HR transformation is a continuous process rather than a single event; consequently, we present each case study as a snapshot of transformation-in-motion rather than the sculpture of a historical hero etched in stone. Since completion of each of the case write-ups, our subject companies have continued to move and change, as they should! The very fact that we begin HR transformation with the business context (see Chapter 2) requires continuous reassessment and renewal as HR drives to deliver organizational capabilities that enable the business to successfully execute its strategy.

- *Flextronics (building from scratch):* We begin our case studies with Flextronics, a $33 billion company that created their strategic HR organization from scratch. In 2006, Flextronics recognized that HR was an essential element to ensuring success in its plans to quadruple revenue over a five-year period. Yet they didn't have a centralized HR function, let alone a strategic one. In the ultimate *tabula rasa* example, follow the fascinating Flextronics story to learn how Paul Humphries and Quinn Wilson built a strategic HR function from the ground up.
- *Pfizer (transforming a large established system):* Our second case highlights extensive work done at Pfizer to radically transform an old, existing HR function to meet business needs in a new, highly competitive environment. Chris Altizer and Michele Bolden explain the process they underwent to separate the strategic from the tactical, focusing their HR professionals on

the most critical work for long-term value-add. Read the Pfizer case to pick up best practices for transforming HR in an established industry leader to meet new business needs.

- *Intel (moving from tactical to strategic):* As a function, HR must transform from tactical to strategic. Our third case specifically describes Intel's push to move from delivering highly effective tactical HR to providing a strong strategic HR capability. Patty Murray and Richard Taylor describe their journey in creating an HR function that maintains sufficient operational excellence while seeking to provide much needed consulting and support to line mangers.

- *Takeda (HR value-add in a small nimble subsidiary):* We conclude our set of case studies with a template of HR transformation in an aggressive entrepreneurial organization seeking to steal market share amidst economic uncertainty. Laurene Bentel and Sandy Mitsch provide an insightful look into the path they led their team on to ensure HR was streamlined and flexible in order to deliver the right organizational capabilities at the right time during a steep growth curve.

FLEXTRONICS: BUILDING A STRATEGIC HR ORGANIZATION FROM SCRATCH

9

Paul Humphries and Quinn Wilson

Although the average consumer may not have heard of Flextronics, most people have used products they manufacture. Flextronics is one of the world's largest electronics manufacturing services (EMS) companies, offering turnkey manufacturing and related services to leading electronics companies. Flextronics' annual report lists its top customers as Cisco Systems, Dell, Hewlett-Packard, and Xerox, among others. In fact, anyone using a brand-name digital camera may be surprised to learn that chances are high that Flextronics produced, designed, and distributed it. From design engineering to manufacturing and assembly, from distribution and warehousing to returns and repairs, Flextronics builds printed circuit boards, electromechanical components, subsystems, and complete systems for a wide range of networking and telecommunications equipment, computers, consumer electronics, and medical instrumentation companies. With revenues exceeding $33 billion in fiscal year 2009 and over 200,000 employees, Flextronics continues to demonstrate its leadership within the EMS industry.

Phase 1: Business Context

From 1993 to 2003, Flextronics leveraged aggressive agility and strategic acquisitions to grow from a $100 million to a $15 billion business, moving from number seventeen to number one in its industry in terms of revenue. At the height of this staggering growth, Flextronics leaders found themselves in the post-9/11 economy managing the largest EMS company in the world.

After the EMS industry stagnated due to the dot-com and telecom crash in 2001, the Flextronics leadership team spent the next four years focused on retaining its position as industry leader by restructuring, closing facilities, and cutting overhead. Despite curbing costs, however, growth plateaued. The prior ten years of dramatic expansion had mainly resulted from fostering an entrepreneurial culture in North American, European, and Asian regional business divisions that functioned quite independently. Meanwhile, the business model was changing for the industry. Customers were asking for more consistent quality and delivery regardless of which region produced their products, and they were looking for services in new locations such as Brazil, Mexico, China, and Hungary.

While Flextronics' North American competitors were facing many of the same challenges, the Taiwanese, who had significantly different business models and who had previously not been considered competitors, were taking market share and growing 20 to 30 percent annually. North American and European competitors were shutting down plants and writing off assets in high-cost regions, while Asian competitors, with very little legacy infrastructure, suddenly had a strong competitive advantage.

Although still the dominant player in the industry in 2006, the Flextronics executive team realized that they needed a new business model to survive—one that better met changing customer requirements while also providing an improved global cost structure. In short, the leadership team determined that Flextronics needed to completely reinvent itself.

To kick off the redesign, the top 150 leaders throughout the company were surveyed to identify the greatest needs in supporting growth and profitability. The survey results recommended the creation of global segments and business units centered on market and product types and supported by a group of centralized global services. Accordingly, where geographically based manufacturing experts previously led the company, new market-savvy presidents were recruited and appointed.

Among the other recommendations, the leadership survey identified the absence of a strategic HR function as a critical barrier to success. Although a multibillion dollar global company, Flextronics did not yet have a centralized HR function and had not effectively aligned the HR function with the business strategy. As the company had acquired plants and equipment, it had also acquired people, and the accumulated HR talent was still functioning as several individual geographically based HR departments whose main focus was on tactical execution and administration of traditional HR activities such as staffing and payroll. Without the necessary focus on a strategic HR capability, including an integrated talent management system and improved organizational effectiveness, Flextronics leaders knew they would not be able to achieve the aggressive growth targets they set.

With a clear understanding of the business realities and recognition that a centralized, strategic HR function would add significant value, the Flextronics executive team appointed Paul Humphries to oversee the creation of a global HR organization. Humphries brought with him an extensive operational and management background from companies such as Borg Warner, AlliedSignal/Honeywell, and Flextronics, as well as HR experience he had acquired earlier in his career at Borg Warner.

Phase 2: Identifying Critical Organizational Capabilities

Humphries and his transformation team had a unique opportunity. Unlike other HR transformation efforts that struggle to nudge an HR organization from "nonstrategic" to "strategic," Humphries had the challenge and luxury of creating an entirely new HR organization from scratch—the proverbial clean slate. Additionally, an HR leader with a nontraditional HR background gave the newly forming function instant credibility with company executives who viewed Humphries as a peer right from the start. As a cohesive team, Humphries, CEO Mike McNamara, and the other members of the strategy team determined that to compete with the Taiwanese upstarts and continue to dominate the industry globally, Flextronics would maintain position through a balance of acquisition and organic growth. As the team detailed Flextronics' new strategy, they agreed on three critical organizational capabilities necessary to support the success of the company's new direction: leadership, customer connectivity, and efficiency.

Leadership

Mike McNamara, who had served as chief operating officer from 2002 to 2005, was named CEO of Flextronics in January 2006. His mission was to architect and lead the global reorganization of the company and provide the organization a clear, longer-term vision. To move quickly from numerous independent divisions to a group of connected, centralized business segments, McNamara and his team determined that consistent leadership would be a key success factor, and they sought to establish a constant pattern of leadership behaviors throughout the organization based on a set of strong company values.

Customer Connectivity

Despite its stagnant growth from 2002 to 2005, in 2006 Flextronics was still doing better than most competitors because the company had shifted from being a pure contract manufacturer to providing integrated services up and down the supply chain. The company expanded into offering design capabilities and began to supply components and the end product, as well as logistics, repair, and distribution services. Flextronics developed vertical integration services, recognizing that customers could be better served by a partner that took on more of the manufacturing process. For example, one customer found significant value in partnering with Flextronics, outsourcing the entire process of digital camera manufacturing from design to distribution. McNamara, Humphries, and other members of the "redesign team" determined that maintaining this customer connectivity would be essential to executing the new strategy.

Efficiency

In addition to leadership and customer connectivity, finding synergies, cutting out waste, improving knowledge sharing across divisions, and producing products better, faster, and at a lower cost was essential for the business to grow and succeed. Moving from a decentralized regional model to a global segment business model required an intense focus on driving efficiencies across the company and around the globe. Consequently, the leadership team chose "efficiency" as one of the three key deliverables to ensure successful implementation of the new strategy.

With a clear understanding of the three organizational capabilities Flextronics needed to succeed (leadership, customer connectivity, and efficiency), Humphries set off to build a global HR organization to strategically support the new direction of Flextronics.

Phase 3: HR Design—Developing the HR Organization, HR Practices, and HR People

The development of a new HR organization began with rigorous benchmarking. Flextronics had the need for solid, aligned global HR programs, yet it was lacking many of them. First steps included talking extensively to universities and attending strategic HR conferences, where Humphries met many people, including Dave Ulrich and representatives from several companies that were eventually benchmarked. From there, Humphries built a small, cohesive HR transformation team, including Richard Wong, VP HR in Asia, and Pat Hehir, SVP Organizational Effectiveness.

HR Strategy

After much deliberation, the HR leadership team determined that the HR strategy would be as follows: Flextronics HR is a strategic business partner responsible for ensuring the business has world-class leadership, develops strong customer connectivity, and operates with leading-edge efficiency. These outcomes are delivered by ensuring a solid organizational structure with a focus on "Design, Discover, and Deliver," which enables a strong focus on talent management; a committed, engaged workforce; and an agile change capability.

The HR strategy team recognized that support for this HR strategy wouldn't be automatic and that communication and buy-in from leaders, HR professionals, and line managers would be essential to sustaining change. To facilitate this communication, the team invited Ulrich to talk at a global leadership summit with 150 senior leaders about the transformation process, what it would take to implement, and the important role a strategic HR function should play in delivering organizational capabilities.

Next, the team cascaded the Flextronics' message of vision, purpose, desired culture, and HR strategy down to the next level of leadership, and then to the next. When all was said and done, Humphries and his senior team personally delivered the message to over fifty sites across four continents. Thousands of line managers and site HR leaders heard from Humphries directly about HR's evolving role in the organization and expectations of HR employees going forward.

HR Organization

In 2005, Flextronics' HR function in the Americas predominantly consisted of professionals focused on compensation, benefits, and HR administration. The HR functions in Mexico and Brazil were essentially site based, and there were disparate country-based HR systems throughout sites in Europe and Asia. There was obvious opportunity to drive considerable improvements in effectiveness of the HR function globally.

Humphries adopted a "Discover, Design, Deliver" HR organizational model. The discover element was comprised of HR business partners who would serve as strategists embedded in the senior leadership teams responsible for each of the global segments/business units. The design element would include multiple centers of excellence in areas such as compensation, learning and development, and HR excellence. Meanwhile, the deliver portion of the model would be the sizeable regional HR operations organizations supporting the three business regions of Asia, Europe, and the Americas. Humphries selected this model for two reasons: first, he wanted a scalable model that would remain cost effective as the organization went through massive growth curves, and second, he wanted to ensure that a strategic element within the function was created to "discover" what would be required by the function to keep it relevant to the business dynamic.

Discover—Building HR Business Partners

The HR transformation team felt it was critical for HR to become an integral part of the new business segments. Given the changing business model and growth initiatives, the team determined that strategic HR support needed to be clearly separated from the tactical support already in place. Quinn Wilson was identified to take the role of Vice President of HR Business Partners to build this strategic HR capability. HR business partners (HRBPs) were for the most part recruited externally and assigned to each business segment. Their mandate included organizational planning and design (including strategy development, goal deployment, organizational design), senior leadership development and coaching (including succession planning, high potential development, 360 coaching), and organizational effectiveness leadership (including change management and team effectiveness). Humphries also looked to them to be cultural custodians, and thus drive and manage the cultural expectations that McNamara and his executives had authored. They were to develop the HR strategy for the segment/business unit they supported and to help senior leaders clearly articulate their business strategy, communicate it to the organization, and align people around it.

To ensure that the HRBPs remained a strategic resource and to reinforce the separation between tactical and strategic, HR leadership created very specific guidelines (rules of engagement and nonnegotiables) around roles and responsibilities. These nonnegotiables provide a healthy "check and balance" system when individual business segment leaders want to create their own customized versions of an HR service. Additionally, as these rules of engagement are explicitly connected to the company's culture, both HR and line managers have increased clarity around HR's purpose and value-add.

Currently, twenty-one experienced HRBPs comprise this functional group, acting as individual contributors and driving the strategic HR focus for the various segments/business units within Flextronics.

Design—Establishing Centers of Excellence and HR Outsourcing

Humphries could see that as Flextronics was evolving quickly, the organization's need for expertise in the areas of staffing, compensation, benefits, learning and development, and M&A were intensifying. The Flextronics HR function clearly needed to develop standardized processes in these specialty areas. To support these needs, centers of excellence (COEs) were created, staffed with subject matter experts who could design broadly applicable, efficient solutions to needs identified by HR business partners and HR operations.

The role of the COEs was to design the central HR processes and systems for business segments, HR operations in local markets, and cultural integration. The HR business partners were to provide input into the design of these processes and systems, and implementation and support for the delivered programs would be handled mainly by HR operations support staff embedded in business segments.

Several strategic COEs were established, including Corporate Social and Environmental Responsibility and Compliance, Total Rewards (compensation and benefits), Learning and Development, Communications, HR Excellence (metrics and process improvement), and Talent Acquisition. In conjunction with external vendors such as Cornerstone and Workday, these COEs developed and introduced global HR management systems utilizing the latest on-demand software to support talent acquisition, performance management, e-learning, compensation programming, and HR data management across all geographical regions.

Deliver—Realignment of HR Operations and Administration

Although the "delivery" organization was in place when Humphries came on the scene, there was a significant need to upgrade senior leadership to rise to the challenge Flextronics' growth curve now presented. For over a year, Humphries spent considerable time reviewing the capability and processes of the regional HR operations organizations. As with the HRBP organization, Humphries sought out solid external talent to improve the bench strength of the HR operations organizations in each of the geographic regions. Numerous acquisitions also brought considerable HR talent to the team, including the Solectron acquisition, which was completed in 2007 and added over fifty thousand employees.

The HR operations function as Humphries envisioned it would be capable of delivering the core of the HR program offerings as well as managing regional and site HR strategy implementation, including employee relations, Corporate Social and Environmental Responsibility initiatives, compliance, and talent acquisition. Currently, each region has a highly competent team in place supporting over two hundred thousand employees in eighty sites globally.

In addition to HR operations professionals, effective HR services and strategies also requires a cost-effective administration. Flextronics uses several specialized systems to manage performance data, hiring processes, benefits enrollment, learning management, and focal processes. Recently, the company began a multiyear project to further improve its administrative capabilities. A global HR shared services strategy is in place and will kick off with the creation of a center in Chennai, India, supporting employees of the

United States and Canada. Similarly, a pilot of shared services is underway in China. Ultimately, Flextronics plans to have several regional centers, operating in support of its workforce across thirty countries.

Additionally, the company is in the first stages of a global HRIS implementation, which will ultimately enable employee self-service, manager self-service, and truly global reporting and data access. Not only will this improve administrative efficiency, but it will also provide greater capability support to HR and management decision making.

Commitment to HR Development

As mentioned above, the new Flextronics business and HR model called for a new type of HR professional at the company. HR leadership leveraged data from the University of Michigan and RBL HR Competency Study to assess competencies the "new HR" professionals needed and how to measure the current employees against those competencies. A career-acceleration training curriculum and competency guidebook were designed to provide behavioral examples of how HR professionals at different career stages and in different HR roles would apply each competency as well as demonstrate how they would be measured. This HR competency model is being deployed as part of the Flextronics HR Capability Enhancement Initiative and will be used for selection, assessment, and development from top to bottom. In sum, while new leaders were brought in from outside the company to jumpstart the HR function, there is a strong push to now grow new leaders internally, with clear career paths, well defined roles, and strategic development opportunities aligned with data-derived competencies.

Phase 4: Accountability and Sustained Change

Perhaps one of the most important elements of Flextronics' HR transformation success was the support of CEO Mike McNamara. Additionally, the support and vision of the senior HR team was essential to attain the progress thus far. Given that this transformation was built from the ground up, the HR team also credits consultants and thought leaders who ensured that the company was employing the latest theory and practice in its new design of HR. Ultimately, there has been an adequately balanced responsibility among line mangers, HR professionals, and external consultants.

Flextronics has also worked to connect its HR practices and people to customers and investors, with a keen interest in ensuring that the design is based on its three designated organizational capabilities: leadership, customer connectivity, and efficiency. Programs are centered on building leaders. Initiatives are implemented with customers' needs at the top of the agenda. Systems and organizations are built to derive the greatest efficiencies.

Next Steps

After three years of significant work, Flextronics has successfully created a global, strategic HR organization and is now operationalizing, executing, and continuing to tweak the design to meet the needs of the ever-changing business. The Flextronics philosophy is that HR transformation work is never fully completed because HR will need to move as the business moves to meet new business challenges. Therefore, although much work has been done, much is left to do. Meanwhile, the progress and success of the HR transformation design work at Flextronics is seen as a significant achievement. Next steps: execution, execution, execution.

CHAPTER 10

PFIZER: A JOURNEY TO SMALLER, BETTER, FASTER

10

Chris Altizer and Michele Bolden

Like many HR functions, Pfizer HR is working to transform itself. Pfizer is behind some companies in this journey and ahead of others. It has gone through significant change in the last several years, and that whole story is too much to tell. We're still writing the story about the implications of those changes for our HR function and its transformation from its traditional personnel and labor focus to a group of business leaders with HR expertise and a lean provider of quality service. But in sharing our story so far with others through the RBL group, we've seen that we have learned some lessons likely to be valuable to those just starting or who aren't satisfied with where they are. Our story doesn't end here and we have much more to do—but we've made a lot of progress.

Phase 1: Business Context

Pfizer is the world's largest pharmaceutical company, but it wasn't always. The company grew rapidly through the 1990s through sales of its own products and through acquisitions, capped by the acquisitions of Warner-Lambert in 2000 and Pharmacia in 2003. The workforce expanded from a base of around 40,000 to 80,000 in 2000, and to 120,000 in 2003. Today, it is 82,000. Through all this, the HR function has met the basic needs of the business, but those basic needs have grown and HR's ability to contribute to and drive the business strategy—high-impact HR work—must be significantly enhanced.

Pfizer is an entrepreneurial and innovative company with a culture to match. While that's good for new product development and marketing, it's a challenge when it comes to striking a balance with standardization and efficiency in support functions. After the Pharmacia acquisition, HR operated in what can be kindly called operational chaos. We had three large legacy companies and an array of different HR practices and systems within divisions within those companies. We had different payroll practices, different pension and benefit plans, different performance and talent practices, and different points of view on the basic role of the function—all on a very large scale.

The result of these differences was an overly large HR function that was unable to deliver quality service at a competitive cost. In addition to its bloated infrastructure, the HR function was short on fresh perspectives and innovative ideas from other environments, as a result of the company's tradition of promoting HR talent from within and of importing talent through acquisition rather than targeted hiring. Most important, the function did not have a track record of driving business results.

The story we're telling here is how we are addressing these issues while supporting a business that is itself being transformed by a changing marketplace, the looming loss of patent protection for products—including for the world's biggest-selling prescription medicine (Lipitor)—and a challenging external environment.

Before sharing the details, it's worth noting that efforts to address these issues had been initiated but were plagued by fits and starts. Pfizer has had four heads of HR since 2000, as well as a new CEO and significant changes to senior management. Despite many plans and some significant progress in some areas, the call to action had been diluted by leadership changes and cultural resistance to accepting a burning platform. The business realities of adapting to a smaller scale and the facts of our own inefficiencies finally came home in 2007.

Business Case for Transformation: The Size of the Prize

To deliver on its commitments to the business, Pfizer HR had to convert itself from a bloated function with an internal focus to an efficient one with a business and industry focus. Table 10.1 shows how performance stacked up against benchmark data from a shareholder and management perspective.

Table 10.1 *Pfizer HR Performance*

METRIC	BEST	MEDIAN	WORST	PFIZER
HR headcount ratio	1:118	1:93	1:67	1:51
HR spending per colleague	$1058	$1611	$2466	$4616
HR revenue percent	0.31	0.51	0.72	0.82

We analyzed our current time allocation and found that over 75 percent of HR interactions were with other HR colleagues, versus work to move the business forward. Historically, we had not had a well-defined HR strategy or operating model that we could credibly say was aligned to the business strategy. Our reputation internally was mixed at best. "I love my HR person, but hate HR," was a common phrase. And when we looked critically, we recognized that our function was not organized for speed, efficiency, or effectiveness.

In early 2007, Mary McLeod joined Pfizer as the head of HR. Over the course of 2007, the HR leadership team (HRLT) determined both our functional aspiration and our plan to get there. Working as a leadership team for perhaps the first time in our collective history, we determined to become a world-class HR function. That's easy to say—we expect every reader of this book says the same—but here's what it means to us:

- Holding HR business leaders accountable for work that helps build Pfizer's competitive advantage with a focus on designing organizations, developing our culture, growing our leaders and other talent, and leading change.
- Ensuring that HR has the talent to design and execute Pfizer's business strategy, support people-related processes and programs, and structure the function to focus on work that enhances Pfizer's competitive advantage.
- Redefining the current relationship between HR, Pfizer leaders, and colleagues. This meant developing new ways of working to help line managers make the most of their time and providing instant access to information through Web-based tools so that business decisions can be made quickly and actions taken instantly to implement those decisions.
- Moving as much routine work as possible to a centralized function where we can standardize it across the company for better quality, easier access, increased speed, and lower cost: HR service *delivery done one way, in one place, by one group.*
- Being known for high performance that drives the desired business results instead of sometimes getting in the way of it.

The aspiration was noble; the challenge was to deliver on it effectively and at a pace to catch up with the company's need for it.

The Plan

We wanted to achieve our goals with as little consultant help as we could manage. We felt we had the talent and the motivation, but needed some help performing the required surgery, as we had never done anything like it before on ourselves. We engaged Mark Nyman of RBL to assist and to keep us honest with ourselves in the early going.

We established three basic design principles to guide the work. The first was accepting the reality that we could not be world class in everything. This was about driving our business as a pharmaceutical company and being best at those things that would do most to drive Pfizer's top five priorities: maximizing revenues, reducing costs, strengthening our culture, meeting our commitments to stakeholders, and engaging our colleagues. A second principle was involvement. The collective brainpower of our HR colleagues was clearly much greater than that of the ten members of the HRLT. We resolved to engage as many of our HR colleagues in this work as practicable, not only to get the benefit of their knowledge but also to build ownership in the outcome. A third principle was the application of the practices and tools of continuous improvement to ensure that our changes were not one-time fixes that would fail to deliver over the three year planning horizon. Figure 10.1 sets out the time line we developed for this work.

Figure 10.1 Pfizer HR Transformation

HORIZON 1
2007

- New SVP of HR appointed
- HRLT begins evolving
- HR Redesign begins; kick-off held
- HR Redesign teams established

HORIZON 2
2008

- HRLT continues to evolve by continuing to strengthen leadership talent with new leaders and new roles
- HR Redesign focuses on defining operating model for how enterprise, divisions, and MOS will work more seamlessly
- New organizations and priorities for diversity and inclusion, talent and organizational capability, and total rewards finalized
- HRLT-1 level announced including HR and MOS leads

HORIZON 3
2009 & BEYOND

- HR Redesign is fully implemented and success measures are realized
- Higher performance realized through the effective implementation of broad-based programs
- Stronger talent pipeline created through the implementation of an integrated talent strategy across Pfizer

HR will be designed effectively and efficiently and have the talent to help lead the growth of business.

We began our approach by identifying the phases of the work, beginning with the needs of the business. We have not yet completed the four phases, but it's useful to lay out our current view of them:

- *Phase 1: Business Context* was essential to understand and help us prepare our business case for initiating an HR transformation. With the size of the prize clearly laid out, we were able to move forward in a much more compelling fashion.
- *Phase 2: Business Outcomes* centers on understanding business unit and enterprise current and future needs, assessing the strategic drivers for each business, and evaluating current and future culture needs. The output is an understanding and agreed-upon list of HR work and implications given the business needs and opportunities for leverage.
- *Phase 3a: Work Classification (HR Redesign I)* centers on identifying outputs, products, or services delivered from HR and determining if the work is strategic or transactional. The expected result from this phase is a comprehensive list of each product and service HR provides and a decision on what products and services should be added, reduced, or eliminated.
- *Phase 3b: Organize the Work (HR Redesign II)* means determining where HR work is best done, which leads to an output of not only how the work should be organized but who owns the work and where it should be done.
- *Phase 3c: The Talent Equation (HR Redesign III)* focuses on ensuring that the right people are in the right positions, understanding the most critical competencies needed for successful HR delivery, and assessing HR talent to identify areas that need upgrading.
- *Phase 4: Implementation* involves determining the speed of delivery, major activities that need to occur, stakeholder management, and building a change management and project plan. The expected outcome is an engaged HR organization whose members are all clear on accountability and how they add value.

Phase 2: Business Outcomes

The HRLT asked our senior leaders to speak to us about the current and future state of the business. We explicitly asked them *not* to talk about HR or what they needed from HR. It was our job to thoroughly understand the needs of the business and for us to build the HR solutions that would drive business success. It was important that we not only look at our company but also at the trends and challenges facing our entire industry if we were to be successful. It was highly engaging and, at times, difficult for leaders to avoid lapsing into HR-speak, but we worked together to clearly outline the business context we needed to start.

Through these discussions, we determined that the new high-end work for HR moves beyond leadership, talent, and culture; it is a matter of deciding what work is needed to help lead the business strategy, organizing the business for its best delivery, and linking the outputs of the business units across the company to achieve results. We began positioning HR not as an enabler of business success but as a driver of it. As this progressed, we began to identify the HR competencies required to do that. The most recent HR competency study conducted by the RBL group and the University of Michigan's Ross School of Business contributed to our thinking and eventually to the new HR competency model—the one we are now in the process of applying.

Phase 3a: Work Classification (HR Redesign I)

With the first two phases complete, we began the third phase—work classification. In talking with other companies, we realized that this phase was most often shortchanged—sometimes with disastrous consequences! Some very respectable companies had gone the route of making assumptions about the work that was done in the function rather than conducting detailed analysis of it. One company we benchmarked had decided to outsource "HR transactional" work to a well-known BPO provider, upgrade its HR talent, and down-size the function to deliver with new efficiency—all at the same time. Because the work had not been classified up front, it emerged that the outsourcer was doing some but not all of the transactional work and that the new, highly skilled HR business partners were still stuck doing the "under-the-table" work that had gone on unnoticed. The HR talent were frustrated to be working below their skill level, the line leaders were not happy, and the high-end HR work was still not getting done. This was a cautionary tale for us.

We created several cross-divisional teams to conduct detailed analysis and to surface the many variations we had across divisions and sites. The initial areas of focus for us were generalist, staffing, learning and development, orga-nizational effectiveness, compensation, benefits, operations, communications, and diversity and inclusion. The initial focus has been on our U.S. operations, which include around 45,000 colleagues over multiple sites and functions. This work was not particularly exciting to do, but the people involved quickly realized what was at stake. The outcome was pages and pages of worksheets showing what work was done and by whom. A key aspect of the work classifi-cation, however, was in determining if each task was "competitive advantage," "strategic," or "foundational."

Briefly put, "competitive advantage" work is the work of the business you are in. For Pfizer, drug discovery, development, marketing, and manufac-turing are competitive advantage work. While initially hard to swallow, we quickly realized that nothing in our current HR work was competitive advan-tage work—that's for Hewitt or RBL or other consulting groups. Our work was either strategic or foundational.

Even that distinction proved to be a challenge, however. No one in HR or anywhere else likes to think their work is not "strategic"—but the fact is that most of our HR work was not. When 75 percent of an HR person's time is spent talking to other HR people, it can't be. Strategic work is the work that enables competitive advantage work. Foundational work is that work that, if not done well, disables competitive advantage work. Contributing to the Asia expansion business plan is strategic work; ensuring people get paid correctly is foundational work. We recognized yet another nuance as well—legally required foundational work. If paying people correctly is foundational, then paying people and ensuring there are no disparities or discrimination is legally required foundational work.

We took the opportunity to help colleagues understand that there's a strategic and foundational aspect to almost everything everyone does. Strategic work is not reserved for senior leaders or change agents, nor is foundational work non-value-added. We had to help colleagues begin to think about the work of HR that way. While these seem like minor distinctions, they became relevant when we began to organize around the work. It took many weeks and was at times confusing, but it was clear to us that accurately classifying the work was fundamental to organizing the work. After we classified the work, we began to determine where it would be done—that is, to organize it.

Phase 3b: Organize the Work (HR Redesign II)

While Pfizer is essentially one large pharmaceutical company with human and animal products, our functions—the commercial, R&D, manufacturing, medical, and corporate groups—are large and diverse enough that we consider them business units (BUs). Historically, much of the HR foundational work was done within the BU HR groups and only in 2003 was a U.S. service center set up. The corporate HR functions were responsible for processes like senior-level talent development, performance management, diversity and inclusion, and compensation, but each BU HR group had similar groups that would use, modify, or sometimes ignore what corporate provided. Once we classified the work (in Phase 2), the facts of our redundancy became starkly apparent and the opportunities for both efficiency and effectiveness became clear.

To ensure focus on the business and prevent redundancy creep, we knew we had to have a structure that would make roles clear. The final design was to include three primary kinds of entities: enterprise, business unit, and manager and operations support (MOS).

Enterprise (Centers of Expertise)

The basic principle is to keep centers of expertise lean and focused on work that impacts the entire company.

- The Compensation and Benefits group develops the corporate philosophy, designs programs, and provides service delivery to the BUs.
- The head of Diversity and Inclusion is responsible for strategy design and for setting objectives and establishing priorities for the D&I colleagues in the divisions.
- HR Planning is responsible for the strategic plan for the function, including the budget and operating plan.
- Talent and Organizational Capability is the center of excellence on talent management and organizational development working with the HR division head and HR line leaders.
- Human Capital Policy is responsible for bringing Pfizer's point of view as an employer to matters of health care and public policy.

Business Unit (Embedded HR)

The basic principle at the BU level is to link HR work closely to that of the business unit.

- BU HR focuses work on organizational and leadership effectiveness, including organizational design, talent planning and development, continuous improvement, change management, workforce planning, engagement, and coaching in the BU.
- The *HR lead* (HR business partner) is accountable for working with a business leader to deliver the business strategy, organizational design and development, change management, workforce planning, continuous improvement, and the talent plan for the BU.
- Analytics and Reporting provides point-of-need HR data and information to drive business decisions.

- BU D&I executes the enterprise diversity and inclusion strategy and priorities at the division and at country levels.
- BU Talent and Organizational Capability executes the training, organizational development and effectiveness, talent acquisition, leadership and talent development tools, processes, and systems in the division.

  Learning and Development work has three major categories: technical training, management development training, and general skill building. BU L&D delivers training and educational needs that are unique to positions within that division.

  Organizational Effectiveness concentrates on team effectiveness and change.

- BU Talent Acquisition will drive the talent acquisition strategy at the divisional level.

Manager and Operations Support (Operational Execution)

The basic principle here is to move as much of the foundational work to manager and operations support as possible.

- Work is located adjacent to the business and efficiently supports organizational and colleague growth.
- Deliver MOS support at the highest level possible: country (minimum) or area or regional (preferred).
- MOS leads colocated at the sites and traditional operations roles centrally located for shared services will be part of this organization.
- MOS work includes performance coaching and improvement plans, compliance investigations, year-end compensation management, on-boarding and off-boarding, workforce compliance training, affirmative action plan development, rollout of new HR processes, and manager coaching; colleagues managing this work will be located at the site adjacent to the business and will report to Operations.

- MOS will continue to manage this work:

  Service center operations
  Payroll and benefits administration
  HR policy and program administration
  HR technology strategy and data management
  Career event administration (leader support)
  Enterprise workforce reporting and analytics

Enterprise and MOS work is done consistently for the entire company; it does not require specific business unit knowledge to execute. Business unit work requires specific BU knowledge and is delivered for a particular business unit across locations.

Exit the Generalist

The HR generalist role as it is done today does not exist going forward. The HR lead will have the responsibility for organizational design and development, change management, workforce planning, continuous improvement, and the talent plan for the business unit. Employee relations work is the responsibility of the manager and operations support staff embedded in the business. The specialist roles in the divisions will have a very close working relationship with the enterprise groups. It is the responsibility of the enterprise groups to design the global programs, and it is the responsibility of the specialist roles to implement those programs in the divisions along with the HR leads.

Phase 3c: The Talent Equation (HR Redesign III)

Shortly after her arrival as head of HR, Mary McLeod set out to upgrade the talent pipeline for the function and identify new value-added work for it. In addition to bringing in a sales VP to head the corporate group's HR function, she brought in top talent to lead the compensation and talent organizations and new leaders for the commercial and R&D HR groups. She established a stronger leadership role across the global function and created the human capital policy function to extend Pfizer's HR influence externally. As the redesign moves into the fourth phase—execution—the task of selecting and deploying the top internal talent and bringing in fresh perspectives across an organization not known for moving HR talent around has presented itself. A major objective has been and remains to put our strongest internal talent in key roles so we have an optimal mix of current and new leaders to perform in the new HR and MOS lead roles.

Using various competency studies including the RBL HR competency work, role profiles were created for the HR and MOS lead positions for each of the divisions. In a first-of-its-kind session (for Pfizer), the HRLT assessed the senior talent bench for the entire organization and selected leaders for these key positions. Unlike better practice companies, we had not been effective to that point at moving talent around the organization for development or to match individual competence to business needs on this scale. We considered several factors, including business and leader continuity, individual strengths and development needs, and the stated intent to leave several key positions open for recruiting top external talent. We have generalists moving into MOS roles and specialists moving into HR lead roles. At press time, those assignments are being executed and a significant shift in HR talent across the enterprise is taking place.

Phase 4: Implementation

In mid-2008, we began executing the redesign. Considering the deadline for this book, the rest of the story will have to be told at a future date. It is worth noting, however, that we will in this design achieve a significant reduction in HR headcount, eliminate approximately $42 million in 2008 expenses through those reductions and through improved project and functional management, and at the same time significantly upgrade the talent base.

This story of classifying and organizing around our work focuses on only one of the paths of our journey. At the same time we are redesigning the HR function, we are also implementing a robust process to prioritize our work so that our entrepreneurial and innovative spirit is focused on the short list of outcomes that will drive the five business priorities outlined earlier—the things we should do rather than those we could do or would find it convenient to do. We intend to continue increasing the business acumen of our HR staff and continue moving and importing HR talent to realize our aspiration of world-class service. All of these steps move us further on the journey.

Next Steps

We will never come to a signpost saying "This Is Success." Instead, success will show up in several ways, including our ability to manage company-wide programs on a global basis in a consistent and efficient way, the ease of delivery in our processes, and our effectiveness in working with business leaders to increase competitive advantage. There are many indicators to choose from, and we have both process and outcome measures. There will be several other indicators as well, including HR staff having more capacity to drive business strategy, change, talent, and culture. The colleague-focused work will be handled one way, in one place, and by one group, which will help us with efficiency and lowering the cost of doing business in HR. The deliverables from the enterprise groups will include being able to drive important people decisions across the company to make the best decisions for the entire company. In combination, these groups will add up to bring the value required of a world-class HR operation to an organization that both deserves and requires it. The strongest indicator of our success will be the level of our involvement in all business decisions about Pfizer's present and future. That may be our next chapter. For the moment, though, the following summarizes our experience:

Early Lessons Learned

A question we get at this point in our journey is about key lessons learned. Set out in detail, they would be their own chapter, if not their own book, but here are a few:

- *Understand the work.* Don't assume you know what gets done, who does it, or what it takes to get it done. Gathering data is hard, but executing without it is impossible.
- *Involve the right people.* Don't delegate the work of transforming the function—but do include the people who will move it forward.
- *Once you start, get it done.* It's taken us a year to do what could have been done in half the time. Beware of being too busy to focus on it or letting the urgent get ahead of the important.
- *Talent is key.* While RBL's recent work tells us that mediocre talent well organized outperforms top talent poorly organized, neither is acceptable. Put your best people on the work and go get the best talent you can find.
- *Deal with the present, focus on the future.* Design structure, define roles, and select talent for the future state; make allowances for current needs only as much as it doesn't (really) disrupt the business—which takes us to the final point . . .
- *This is neither easy nor seamless.* No one will get everything they want, and the transition will be messy. Set expectations for your business leaders, but don't seek permission or think they will drive or "sponsor" it. They have a business to run and so do you. Run it.

CHAPTER 11

INTEL: SWINGING THE PENDULUM FROM TACTICAL TO STRATEGIC

11

Richard Taylor and Patty Murray

Intel Corporation is the world's largest semiconductor company and the inventor of the microprocessors found in most personal computers. Intel was founded in 1968 by semiconductor pioneers Robert Noyce, who was inducted into the Inventors Hall of Fame in 1983, and Gordon Moore, who is well-known for "Moore's Law" (which states that the number of transistors incorporated in a chip will approximately double every 24 months). Intel also makes motherboard chipsets, network cards, integrated circuits, flash memory, graphic chips, embedded processors, and other devices related to communications and computing. The third employee hired at Intel was Andrew Grove, who led the company through the 1980s and 1990s, combining advanced chip design capability with a leading-edge manufacturing capability. Intel has continued to grow through the 2000s, and in recent years has continued its legacy of innovation by building a strategic HR function capable of leveraging the best talent to deliver the most innovative technology.

Phase 1: History and Business Context

In 1999, one of Intel's finance executives was waiting in the airport for a flight when he saw a friend from payroll. In conversation, the executive asked his associate where he was headed. The response left the executive flabbergasted. Came the sheepish reply, "Well, I'm hand-delivering a box full of payroll checks because our systems jammed up and we weren't able to get the checks out!"

While hand-delivered checks might have been the norm for a traditional industrial company, this was unacceptable at the world's largest semiconductor company. As the story quickly made its way to other senior executives, HR was given a stern mandate to right the ship.

In HR's defense, Intel was experiencing both significant organic growth and expansion through acquisition. Business needs were evolving rapidly, and employee expectations were high and constantly increasing. Additionally, technology capabilities were rapidly evolving, the paperless office, B2B exchanges, and e-commerce were blasting off, and Intel's operation capabilities were not keeping pace with technology or needs. In essence, while most HR organizations have the luxury of evolving at a slower pace, Moore's Law was spilling out of R&D and into every function within Intel, especially into HR: *everything* was doubling, not just transistors on chips. With all the changes, HR leaders experienced the very painful realization that basic HR services and benefits operations were struggling to keep pace with the company's phenomenal growth and were falling behind the expectations of customers.

Despite the concerns and need for improvement, as the world glided smoothly through the much-hyped Y2K and into the new century, Intel's HR team felt they had a handle on the situation. The calm before the storm was July 2000 when Intel's stock hit $64 per share and split 2:1. Three months later, the stock price had dropped in overall value by over 30 percent per share along with the rest of the industry, and Intel began to feel the pressure of the dot-com bust. We began to scrutinize every aspect of HR service delivery and found multiple areas for improvement. Our compensation and benefits plans were complex, customized, and not designed for ease of administration. Our service solutions were fragmented and manual. Our systems were highly customized and not well integrated, and our focus was on simply completing transactions. We found we were delivering poor quality (~100K DPM—that is, 100,000 defects-per-million opportunities), at high cost (fourth quartile-versus industry-average HR spend), and with low satisfaction among our internal customers (65–85 percent). Meanwhile, the broader HR organization was divided into heavily siloed areas; the HR organizational culture was reactive and lacking fundamentals such as managing with data, project management, and supplier management capabilities; and we had gaps in our management capabilities, depth of expertise, and business and technical skills.

We found that our initial reaction (from 1999 to 2001) to the mandate from Andy Grove (then chairman of the board) and Craig Barrett (then CEO) to upgrade HR resulted in a lot of wheel spinning with relatively little traction. We were investing heavily in HR services and our spending had grown at a rate of 41 percent per year. However, we were making little progress; all our investments were single-point reactions to specific problems, and few if any addressed root causes or embodied an overarching strategy.

Given the cost pressures of the external environment and Intel's data and technology culture, Grove and Barrett agreed with our plan to focus intensely on the basics. From 2001 through 2006, we concentrated on fixing the foundation of service delivery. Through this five-year period, we thoughtfully and purposefully made dramatic progress. We started by creating a single HR services organization with a comprehensive global strategy, targeting the right skills. We then systematically worked through all the individual functions, standardizing and reengineering our core processes. Our processes were built on an integrated technical infrastructure with one global system of record, robust automation, and quality Web tools. Additionally, we outsourced key e-HR work and implemented formal supplier and project management procedures. By 2006, our HR services had a solid foundation. Technology, process, and line manager tools were so well streamlined that one employee exclaimed, "I was hired to work in the Intel marketing department in 2004 and I never had to talk to an HR person for two years! The staffing process, payroll, benefits, and performance management all worked smoothly. If I had any questions, I knew I could find answers either online or through my manager."

Looking back across the years of improvement, the breadth and depth of positive change in the organization was immense. The HR culture was transformed. We were now a proactive organization with a penchant for managing with data. We fixed our quality problems to typically better than 2K DPM (a dramatic 98 percent reduction), and our internal customer satisfaction rating was routinely better than 90 percent. And while we did make progress on cost during this time, cost was not our primary focus. For HR, 2001 through the beginning of 2006 were years focused on world-class services, targeting best-in-class quality and impeccable customer satisfaction.

However, Intel faced increasing competitive pressure as the company continued to grow in emerging markets and sell more product in developing economies. In January 2006, when Intel failed to meet analysts' and its own expectations for revenue and earnings for 2005, Intel joined Yahoo and other technology bellwethers in a shocking stock drop of more than 15 percent. The stock continued to decline throughout the first quarter of 2006, and the Intel leadership team knew they had to jump-start growth. By June 2006, the stock had dropped 35 percent from its peak in December of the preceding year. However, the leadership team began to take action that same month when Intel announced it would be shipping a new chip, the Xeon processor 5100, to power network servers. Intel also announced that it would sell off a division that made processors for handheld devices to Marvell Technology in a $600 million deal. The divestiture to Marvell was part of a larger restructuring plan, and after several months of intense analysis during the summer of 2006, the leadership team was ready to execute its plan to radically change Intel in pursuit of a lower cost structure and greater nimbleness and efficiency.

On September 5, 2006, Intel announced plans for a major restructuring, including a reduction of 10,500 jobs. As a result of the restructuring, Intel would generate savings in costs and operating expenses of approximately $3 billion annually by 2008. In addition, Intel hoped to achieve a capital expenditure avoidance of $1 billion by making better use of manufacturing equipment and space. The savings would be a combination of non-workforce-related steps and a significant reduction in Intel's workforce.

HR had made major strides since the executive's chance encounter with his friend from payroll in the airport eight years earlier. With increased confidence in HR's ability to deliver tactical results, there was now a clear business case for HR to transform from a high-performing transactional organization to a highly strategic organization.

Phase 2: Desired Outcomes

As we prepared to announce Intel's restructuring, we participated in a series of strategic discussions to determine the critical capabilities Intel would need to grow into the future. An obvious outcome for all our investors was to reduce costs and improve our balance sheet. Although cost reduction was a must, however, we realized that a strategy based on reducing costs would be disastrous in our industry. To ensure the company would be able to deliver long-term results for all of its stakeholders (investors, customers, employees, and communities), we went back to our roots. We realized that to truly grow in the future, we would need to continue to deliver on Moore's Law and ensure the organizational capability of fast innovation. Additionally, from the founders (who both were Ph.D.s) to our engineers, operations leaders, and marketers, we had always been a very bright and educated group. We realized that we would need to continue to improve our ability to attract, engage, and retain brilliant talent. Finally, while Intel had always been a collaborative environment, we determined to focus on increasing collaboration and demanding a large degree of initiative in that collaboration.

In addition to the tactical work HR was already delivering well, HR had a new job: to enable capabilities in fast innovation, brilliant talent, and proactive collaboration. To do so, we realized that we would need to reduce the cost and complexity of our tactical delivery and begin to develop a strategic HR competency among our HR professionals.

Phase 3: HR Redesign

Before doing anything, we had to fine-tune our HR strategy to fit with the strategy of the organization going forward. We felt that our initial vision and mission were basically in line, so we adjusted our strategic model given the new circumstances. As is the case with any support function in a rapidly changing industry, strategy adjustments are driven by a confluence of forces. We realized that in our new strategy we not only had to go on delivering HR services well, we had to deliver HR services that enabled proactive collaboration, brilliant talent, and fast innovation.

HR Organization

With the new strategy in mind, we adjusted our structure and resource allocation to promote the desired outcomes of each transformational wave. Over the previous several years, we had focused the organizational structure on chartering additional resources to improve knowledge and information flow between heavily siloed organizations, to improve fundamentals such as managing with data, and to manage projects. All augmentations and budget increases had been well planned and thoughtfully placed as we systematically set about filling gaps in our management capabilities and depth, and in our business and technical skills.

Now, in the new business context, the top-down restructuring and strategic initiatives drove our HR transformation strategy. We adjusted our structure and resource allocation to the desired outcomes. We formed a new unified organization with a tri-part structure: a strategic design group, a business channel group, and a HR operations group:

- *The Strategic Programs and Design Groups* are charged with designing hallmark programs that give Intel a competitive edge. The team focuses on long-range HR strategy in developing our desired organizational capabilities of talent, collaboration, and innovation by leveraging diversity, talent management and acquisition, and compensation and benefits. This organization is similar to the "centers of expertise" developed in other companies; however, a unique design element is the inherent collaboration built into the way the groups function. By seeking to foster innovation and collaboration within our own organization, we hope to create practices and policies around key HR practices that do the same.

- *The Business-Facing Channel* was charged with providing the HR partnership role into the company's business units. These are the business partners responsible for organizational development, employee relations, strategic business partnering, analytics, and program rollout. This was a key area where we found we needed to upgrade our skill set. Many of our HR people were very good at tactical execution, project management, and program delivery, but we found a gap in analytical and consulting skills. In many cases, we simply had to hire new talent into the organization to fulfill the business partner role.

- *The Operations Group* was charged with delivering all HR services, including pay, benefits, training, staffing, and relocation and travel. This group inherited the bulk of the work we had done in past years. Given the cost pressures and recently focused strategic direction, we had to realign demand and service levels, standardize and rationalize many systems, and reduce complexity. Ultimately, this group was held responsible for delivering shareholder value by reducing the annual cost structure by $100 million. Despite the tremendous work done up until 2006, the Operations Group faced quite a task; they had to continue delivering high quality with reasonable customer satisfaction at a cost approaching the first-quartile benchmark.

With the three key areas outlined, we realigned programs, resources, and tasks to the appropriate organization. Additionally, we integrated HR and training resources that had previously reported into Intel business units; conversely, we repatriated finance, IT, and other resources that had been reporting with the HR function to their respective organizations. Given the extreme business conditions and the 10,500-position reduction, we were forced to dramatically reduce resources in all three HR divisions, and work that was not perceived as strategic or essential to business operations was eliminated. These were extremely difficult decisions, but they had to be made to right the ship. We established a goal that puts the ratio of human resource professionals to overall Intel employees at 1:55, a ratio lean enough to be effective but not so lean as to hinder quality of service and partnership.

HR Practices

As noted, the Operations Group is responsible for modifying our HR practices to use fewer resources and put an increased focus on innovation, talent, and collaboration. Unlike the typical activity you might see in other organizations going through HR transformation, we found ourselves actually downgrading many of our HR practices. Over the years and with thicker budgets, we had developed world-class practices that, although nice to have, didn't necessarily provide the company with a competitive advantage. Given the need to reduce costs and to put more resources into HR activities that would increase our competitive advantage, we found that we had to live with a higher DPM rate and a lower "internal customer satisfaction" rate. The result in 2007 and 2008 has been an expected decrease in employee and manager satisfaction on many of the common tactical HR measures.

Nonetheless, our HR Operations Group continues to push improvements in two main areas: focus on business outcomes and priorities, and elimination of bureaucracy and facilitation of transparency using metrics and dashboards to deliver data directly to the managers. For example, while we have been doing less hiring, we have emphasized ideas like the Rotation Engineer Program, which have allowed us to focus our hiring on the best and the brightest. We have also focused on leveraging technology to drive global collaboration (for example, among other initiatives, we have worked with other business leaders to create several telepresence rooms). HR has also focused on delivering services that have supported the development of the Quad-Core, the GT200, the RV770, and even the Atom processor built with the world's smallest transistors and manufactured on Intel's industry-leading 45nm Hi-k Metal Gate technology. The Intel Atom processor was purpose-built for simple, affordable "netbooks" and "nettops." In essence, while we have had to make a number of difficult choices, we are pleased to see that the areas we are focusing on are delivering value for our external customers by driving innovation, a focus on brilliant talent, and increased collaboration in our product development teams.

HR People

Our HR competencies and roles have certainly changed in conjunction with our HR transformation. Our effort to increase HR operational excellence from 2001 to 2006 brought to the fore project management capabilities, process engineering, vendor relationship management, business partnership, total quality, Six Sigma, communications, and data analytics and reporting. Now our transformation from tactical to strategic has brought to the fore the business-facing HR organization, where we initiated major changes to up-level the work of HR professionals away from the transactional and task-oriented toward strategic value-added capabilities. We moved HR business professionals to a single job family with generalist skills focused on organizational development, employee relations, strategic business partnership, analytics, and program rollout. We also limited HR support to the most senior level within each business group. We realigned regional resources. Finally, we federalized embedded HR resources throughout the enterprise.

We orchestrated the change in rigorous analytical processes to define the current state and the gap between where we are and the desired end state. During these diagnostics, we also took immediate action, prioritizing and picking off quick wins for maximum impact. Following the diagnostics, we implemented solutions according to a set of functionally integrated road maps. Throughout, we kept a steady stream of communication to our stakeholders. In summary, competencies changed consistent with each transformational wave. We thoroughly evaluated all roles, adding, deleting, mapping, and aligning roles to the new strategic vectors and expectations. We evaluated each employee against new skill sets. We thoughtfully managed and orchestrated change. Communication of the strategy, organizational changes, new expectations, and transition plans occurred at all levels beginning with the VPs of HR, each HR business unit, and each HR organization through open forums, all-hands meetings, informal brown-bag lunches, blogs, webcasts, and e-mail blasts.

In addition to looking at competencies, we have taken a focused look at the background and experiences of our HR team, with the intent to balance a specific mix of people working in HR. We have sought to balance our HR population with one-third coming from traditional HR backgrounds, one-third coming from other analytical functions (operations, engineering, finance, legal, and so on) and one-third from external disciplines, including consultants, anthropologists, and other scholars. A significant benefit from this is that each of the three groups brings its own network into the HR function. As we seek out individuals from different functions, we have developed a "seed operation" recruiting process, where we find high-performing, high-potential individuals from other functions to bring into HR, and then encourage them to bring their best people from elsewhere in the organization. The result is that HR credibility has risen significantly.

As with almost any approach, of course, we've encountered some pitfalls. For example, just as it can be difficult to develop business analytics skills among some HR people, it turns out that not just any engineer can perform well in an HR position. Nonetheless, we are finding great success as we tighten up our selection and training efforts to address these issues.

Phase 4: Implementation and Accountability

Over the last two years, line management supported each wave of HR transformation by evaluating resources against new roles and responsibilities; selecting, deselecting, and prioritizing tasks; and communicating and managing change within their groups. As we began our transformation, we developed four key areas of focus and collaboration with line managers: change management discipline, stakeholder management processes, employee communication tools and support, and transition management rigor.

Granted, this work hasn't been without some concerns and frustration, including feedback that the planning and transformation implementation has lasted too long and that changes were not immediate but continuous, over an extended period of time. Some feel that the HR transformation has had a negative impact on the organization's health. However, seeing the positive impact on business results by HR leaders who are more strategic has generated a positive reaction as HR's reputation continues to evolve.

Ultimately, we believe that our HR transformation has been a success and that we have achieved the quality, satisfaction, and financial results we intended, with no interruption to service levels. Additionally, the HR organization has successfully managed through its own organizational changes while supporting the company through its transitions.

Next Steps

We have come a long way at Intel, and we certainly have a long way to go. We have found success through best practices of solid data management, a strong project management discipline, identifying and adjusting the right skill and service levels, and garnering strong support from the CEO and other key executives. Going forward, we aim to continue focusing managing the paradox of reducing costs while increasing employee development and engagement. With a focus on our strategic capabilities of innovation, talent, and collaboration, we believe we can continue the constant journey to deliver value for the business through HR.

CHAPTER 12

TAKEDA NORTH AMERICA: CREATING CAPABILITY IN A FAST-TRACK SUBSIDIARY

12

Laurene Bentel and Sandy Mitsch

Background

Over two centuries ago, a small medicine shop was opened in Doshomachi, Osaka, Japan, to provide medicines to local merchants and doctors. This was the beginning of the present-day Takeda Pharmaceutical Company Limited, Japan's largest pharmaceutical company. Many generations later, in 1998, Takeda Pharmaceuticals North America, Inc. (TPNA), was created as a wholly owned subsidiary of Takeda Pharmaceutical Company Limited.

Founded to accelerate Takeda's global expansion into the U.S. market, TPNA started with three employees and now employs more than 5,000 people. TPNA was built on the introduction of ACTOS®, an oral antidiabetes drug. Our mission is simple and compelling: We are dedicated to serving patients by providing innovative products that improve their lives with better healthcare. Our commitment to patients, employees, partners, and the larger community gives us the purpose to build on the tremendous success we enjoy as one of the top fifteen pharmaceutical companies in the United States. We present this chapter as a unique perspective of HR transformation in a small but growing subsidiary of a large international firm.

---

*Editor's note: The case story presented is based on the company's HR initiative in 2006–2007. In 2008, TAP Pharmaceutical Products, Inc., merged with TPNA and Takeda Global Research and Development Center to form today's company, which has an even larger employee base and portfolio of products.

Phase 1: Business Context

Thanks to the early success of ACTOS®, our North American business experienced unprecedented growth between 1998 and 2005. However, with growth based primarily on one key drug and the whole industry facing increased pressure to come up with innovative products and new solutions against global competition, the TPNA leadership team drafted a strategy to move quickly from a single product to a multiproduct portfolio. Beginning in 2005, TPNA began launching several additional drugs, including Duetact® and ROZEREM®. Each of these launches required numerous resources and a detailed focus on the market to keep the pressing pace and grow market share. Meanwhile, TPNA leaders found themselves competing for talent among pharmaceutical companies, which added intense pressure to attract and retain top-quality leaders.

As with any start-up, HR's original responsibility was to simply get the basics right. Given the rapid growth, however, relatively straightforward transactional work such as compensation and benefits suddenly became mission critical as staff grew from a few hundred initial employees to thousands over the course of a few years. In one market, for example, we found ourselves faced with the demand from TPNA leaders to hire over five hundred sales representatives in one quarter. By January 2006, a new HR leadership team was formed and quickly acknowledged that HR needed to move from a traditional transactional HR organization to a strategic, business-oriented organization to support this same rate of growth in the coming years.

Phase 2: Outcomes

Given the customer needs and increasing demands from business leaders to deliver value, the HR leadership team gathered for an off-site meeting in early 2006 to reset the HR strategy. Our goal was to develop a strategy that provided for a more business-oriented, less transaction-driven HR group to help business leaders achieve their talent and organizational needs over the next five years of growth.

Our team realized that more data was needed to ensure strong alignment with business leaders. We determined to follow a two-phase approach to strategy development. First, we interviewed executives and their management teams from our commercial business and support functions to gather strategy perceptions, perspectives, and customer needs. Next, we facilitated an organizational capability audit as outlined by Ulrich and Smallwood in the 2004 *Harvard Business Review* article "Capitalizing on Capabilities."

- *Talent:* Of the many capabilities on which we could focus, our interviews and audit identified talent as one of the most critical capabilities for TPNA's success. As we aimed to continue rapid growth in a very entrepreneurial environment, we needed experienced people who could hit the ground running with a high tolerance for ambiguity and change. Our business unit was still relatively small and our parent company allowed us quite a bit of flexibility—assuming that certain goals were achieved. This led to an aggressive start-up mentality with business leaders in all functions relying on self-starters who could thrive amid uncertainty while creating processes and policies necessary to meet customer needs. Audit findings also revealed a need for a more diverse set of skills and backgrounds than we had at the time. Our team was confident that if HR could create strong talent capability for our budding business, many of our other barriers to growth would be resolved.
- *Accountability:* The second capability that required additional focus was accountability. To compete as a small fish in the large pond of North American pharmaceutical companies, we determined to build a solid, performance-driven culture. Business leaders agreed that a focus on accountability for delivering both results *and* demonstrating company values would balance the entrepreneurial culture and ensure quality and safety for our customers. Given that HR had traditionally provided transactional support to business leaders, we agreed that evolving our performance appraisal and decision-making practices to a higher standard would be a natural and important move. Ultimately, we knew that we needed to be good at creating and enforc-

ing standards that lead to high performance and execution to maintain our high growth model.

- *Innovation:* Survival for pharmaceutical companies is largely dependant on ensuring a steady pipeline of new and differentiated drug candidates. Along with the talent we needed to do the work, and accountability to ensure work was done right, we concluded that a third critical organizational capability for TPNA was innovation. Developing a strong innovation capability had obvious implications for our research and development teams. However, we also realized that to continue to take market share from bigger competitors we would find success if every employee throughout the organization was good at improving on current processes and developing new cross-functional processes when needed.

Once we identified the business outcomes critical to TPNA's success, we now had the task of creating an HR function to deliver talent, accountability, and innovation.

Phase 3: HR Redesign

What began as an effort to better understand client needs and align existing HR professionals to those needs in 2006 grew into a full-scale transformation by early 2007. By the time we had completed the interviews and identified our three target organizational capabilities (talent, accountability, and innovation), motivation had greatly increased within both the HR team and our business leaders to begin the redesign phase. We determined that transformation for TPNA HR would be a complete system change, involving not only greater partnering with line business leaders, but also making internal changes to better align the HR department with the business strategy. This systemic change affecting the core HR vision and processes translated into a new HR strategy based on delivering organizational capabilities to drive business growth.

HR Organization, Practices, and People

Given the size of our HR organization and our desire to maintain flexibility to accommodate our business plans, we structured our organization to include a Talent Management center of excellence, an Employee Experience Group designed to absorb operational HR work, and a group of HR business partners tasked with enabling strategic execution by line and functional managers.

Center of Excellence—Talent Management Group

With a keen focus on developing our talent capability, we brought our staffing, training, and performance management groups together under one umbrella, named the Talent Management Group. The group's mission was to manage the employee lifecycle from prehire, onboarding, and early developmental experiences through to leadership development and succession planning.

Business leaders readily accepted the increased strategic focus on talent and welcomed our Talent Management Group leaders' participation during the business planning process. Our group leaders facilitated discussions to assess the human capital needs for each function, how they would be utilized, and how to maximize the talent in current roles. We also outlined the short- and long-term savings from strategic talent management as opposed to the reactive approach of filling open positions quickly and ignoring the impact of poor hiring on the business. Initial engagement with business leaders was favorably received and led to additional requests from top management.

Meanwhile, performance competencies were aligned with our organizational capabilities, and, in turn, our learning and development programs were refocused to better align with our competencies. The net result was a targeted development approach tied directly to results and our performance management process. Guided by one leader with a strategic view, the Talent Management Group found synergies in combining our staffing, training, and performance management teams and became the collaborative group connecting at all the key points of the employee lifecycle.

Operational HR—Employee Experience Group

Our second group was created to align communications, organizational effectiveness, employee engagement, and the benefits team. One key result was an in-sourced Employee Resource Center (ERC) with a mandate to provide experienced high-touch service—supporting our focus on talent—while driving efficiencies in the delivery model.

Meanwhile, a number of HR generalists who had previously been assigned to handle employee inquiries and similar tactical concerns were freed up to do more strategic work. The ERC became the first point of contact for all employee questions coming into HR and changed the mindset of employees throughout the organization. We launched the ERC with a strategic communication initiative and employees quickly became aware of where to go for everyday answers to their questions, thus replacing the bulk of the work previously done by our HR generalists while increasing the level of satisfaction. Our operations team continues efforts to make the transactional work more efficient through HR systems support and payroll and benefits processing. The broader Employee Experience team provided the data (organizational effectiveness and engagement), the services (ERC), and the messaging (communications) to enhance the overall employee experience.

Embedded HR—Strategic Business Partners

In an important phase of the reorganization, HR generalists with the right skill sets were repositioned to play more strategic roles and their jobs were redefined as "HR business partners." In addition to HR expertise, these business partners were required to have excellent listening and consulting skills, along with solid business acumen and a strong financial background.

Corporate HR

Given the creation of our business partner role, the employee experience group, and the Talent Management Group, we agreed to maintain a very small HR leadership team at TPNA. Our corporate HR leader in Japan, who consulted on the changes throughout the process, was generous in allowing a great deal of flexibility and trust regarding the changes being made, which allowed the process to move forward quickly.

Realigning HR Professionals

As we progressed from diagnosis to the new structure, one of the critical questions that had to be answered was to what extent we felt the current HR leaders had the capabilities to function in the newly defined roles. After the structure was identified, our HR leadership team held a very intense session reviewing the strengths and development opportunities of each of our HR professionals. Assumptions were checked and double-checked, and then moves were announced. We helped many employees retool, brought in new talent from outside the organization, and helped a handful of employees transition, both internally and externally, because their skill sets didn't match our newly defined organizational needs. The net result is an organization where our HR talent is considered a shared resource and honesty and candor are more commonplace.

Phase 4: Accountability and Ongoing Communication

Keeping everyone informed during times of change, especially when changes directly affected individual jobs, was an essential tenet of our HR transformation process. One of our methods to keep our stakeholders involved throughout the process was to build on our initial executive interviews and hold a regular stakeholder meeting with updates on our work, our intended next steps, and expectations of roles and responsibilities. Additionally, we were guided throughout the transformation by external consultants from the RBL Group. In addition to capitalizing on coaching from Jon Younger and others during each step in the process, we leveraged Jon's expertise to increase credibility with our leadership team and external stakeholders by providing best-practice benchmarks and the latest research on the changing role of HR.

Next Steps

Since we completed our first round of HR transformation, the business has continued to evolve with a significant merger, acquisitions, and a global corporate organizational restructure. As a result, HR continues to evolve as we look at ways to support the ever-changing business and operate more efficiently. Looking back, our focus on talent has proven to be the most meaningful piece of our work and has contributed greatly to our success and ability to continue both acquired and organic growth. Our organization's capability to ensure accountability and deliver innovation has improved as well. Meanwhile, although we have already achieved many of our desired outcomes, we continue to reassess our approach in the spirit of continuous improvement and look forward to future growth and continued transformation.

HR TRANSFORMATION TOOLKIT

In an effort to make HR Transformation as practical as possible, and to ground our theory in best practice examples and proven processes, we have compiled the following tools which can be found at www.TransformHR .com. We trust that these will prove helpful aids in the journey of sustainable transformation.

CHAPTER 1

TOOL 1.1 | *Full Virus List*

In our work on managing change, we have identified more than 30 common viruses—common reasons why change does not proceed as intended. Download the full list of organizational viruses and learn more about virus busting.

TOOL 1.2 | *HR Transformation Model Overview*

Watch a video of Dave Ulrich introducing the HR transformation model. Learn as he grounds this theory in reality with examples of how companies have implemented each phase of the model.

CHAPTER 2

TOOL 2.1 | *HR Transformation Readiness Assessment*

Are you ready for HR transformation? Invite your entire team to complete the full HR Transformation Readiness assessment online to determine if it's time for you to begin HR transformation.

▶ *Go to **www.TransformHR.com** to access these tools.*

TOOL 2.2 | *Preparing for HR Transformation*

Learn from Jon Younger as he describes how to create the conditions you need to initiate a successful HR transformation and shares best practices in HR transformation preparation. Share this video with your team during your transformation kick-off meeting.

TOOL 2.3 | *HR Transformation Jumpstart Methods*

Download additional ideas and approaches when launching an HR transformation initiative.

TOOL 2.4 | *Stakeholder Analysis*

Be very clear to ensure your stakeholders' expectations and needs are addressed at the beginning and are embedded in everything you do throughout the HR transformation. Download and print the Stakeholder Analysis Worksheets. Have your entire team complete the worksheet, then prioritize stakeholder needs.

TOOL 2.5 | *External Environment*

Understanding the complexities in your external environment is critical to a sustainable HR transformation. Watch Wayne Brockbank explain the impact of external environment on successful transformation.

TOOL 2.6 | *Business Case Worksheet*

Download a copy of the business case worksheet. Encourage each member of the HR transformation team to complete the worksheet prior to holding your business case development meeting.

▶ *Go to* **www.TransformHR.com** *to access these tools.*

TOOL 2.7 | *HR Transformation Business Case*

Watch Justin Allen describe a process for developing a transformation business case and listen as he shares examples of transformation teams who have successfully communicated their business case to the Board of Directors, the senior executive team, the HR leadership team, and HR professionals throughout the organization.

CHAPTER 3

TOOL 3.1 | *Organizational Capabilities*

Watch a video of Dave Ulrich explaining the importance of organizational capabilities and why they are HR's number one deliverable.

TOOL 3.2 | *Organizational Capability Assessment*

Be sure your HR transformation team is clear about the capabilities your organization needs. Check out the RBL Organizational Capability Assessment.

TOOL 3.3 | *Operationalizing Your Capabilities*

Turn the capabilities identified in the capability audit into specific measures that can be monitored and tracked. Watch a video of Mark Nyman describing how to connect the deliverables of the transformation in a scorecard such that everyone knows the desired results and how well the organization is meeting those results.

TOOL 3.4 | *Mapping Capabilities to Stakeholders*

Listen to Justin Allen share best-practice examples of how to show that the development of your key capabilities will benefit employees, line managers, customers, investors, communities, and other stakeholders.

CHAPTER 4

TOOL 4.1 | *HR Strategy Statement*

Download a copy of the HR Strategy Statement Worksheet and use this document as a template in your HR strategy clarification meeting.

TOOL 4.2 | *Drafting a Powerful HR Strategy*

Learn from Wayne Brockbank as he describes how to draft an HR strategy and then how to make it real.

TOOL 4.3 | *Strategic vs. Transactional Work*

As seen in the Pfizer case (see chapter 10) separating transactional from transformational work is an essential step in any HR transformation. Listen to Mark Nyman describe the sifting process.

CHAPTER 5

TOOL 5.1 | *The Six Bs Overview*

Obtain more information about the Six Bs and other resources that can help you align your HR practices with your business strategy.

TOOL 5.2 | *VOI²C²E Overview*

Obtain more information about using the VOI²C²E model and other resources that can help you bolster and strengthen your employees such that they strengthen others.

TOOL 5.3 | *Strategy Assessement Worksheet*

Download a copy of the Strategy Assessment Worksheet.

▶ *Go to **www.TransformHR.com** to access these tools.*

TOOL 5.4 | *Transforming HR Practices*

Listen to Jon Younger describe how he has helped many HR
departments transform their practices to align with customer needs.
In particular, listen to Jon's unique perspective on how to link talent
to customers.

CHAPTER 6

TOOL 6.1 | *HR Competencies Overview*

Over the last 20 years, Dave Ulrich and Wayne Brockbank have
gathered the world's largest database on HR competencies that
positively impact business success. Listen to Wayne describe the
results of the latest round of data collection and the implications for
HR professionals.

TOOL 6.2 | *HR Competencies Research*

Download a concise summary of the RBL / University of Michigan HR
Competencies study as well as the first chapter of the *HR Competencies* (2008) book.

TOOL 6.3 | *HR Competencies Assessments*

Ensure that you are focused on developing the right skills for your HR
professionals by assessing them and then comparing data from your
organization with global norms. Download a sample report of the RBL
HR Competencies 360 Assessment.

TOOL 6.4 | *Strategic HR Professional Development*

Effective development of HR professionals involves interventions in
three key categories: work experience, life experience, and formal
training/mentoring. Learn from leading global organizations as Justin
Allen shares best practices in sustainable leadership development.

CHAPTER 7

TOOL 7.1 | *Building an HR Transformation Team (internal)*

Building the HR transformation team is critical for effective execution and long-term success. Listen to Mark Nyman describe who should be on the team from HR and line management and critical roles that must be played.

TOOL 7.2 | *Building an HR Transformation Team (external)*

Now that you've decided who from HR and line management should be on your HR transformation team, how are you going to involve customers, investors and external thought leaders? Listen to Jon Younger describe essential external roles for HR transformation.

CHAPTER 8

TOOL 8.1 | *HR Transformation Milestones Checklist*

Use the HR Transformation Milestones Checklist as a guide throughout your transformation process. Download a printable copy of the Milestones Checklist.

TOOL 8.2 | *Pilot's Checklist*

Download a printable copy of the Pilot's Checklist and learn more about resources for sustainable change management.

TOOL 8.3 | *Accountability and Change Video*

You've read the book; now it's time to make change happen. Listen to Dave Ulrich's closing remarks and charge to the HR profession.

▶ *Go to **www.TransformHR.com** to access these tools.*

REFERENCES AND RECOMMENDED READING

We are grateful and indebted to our colleagues who have informed our thinking. This section first provides biographical information for the works we cited throughout the book. Next we offer a list of our "favorites" for those readers who wish to continue to obtain a more detailed understanding of topics within the four HR transformation phases.

References

Chapter 2

McGahan, Anita M., and Michael E. Porter. "How Much Does Industry Matter, Really?" *Strategic Management Journal* 18, no. S1 (1997): 15–30.

Ulrich, Dave, and Norm Smallwood. *How Leaders Build Value*. Hoboken, NJ: Wiley, 2006.

Chapter 3

Ulrich, Dave, and Norm Smallwood. *Leadership Brand*. Boston: Harvard Business School Press, 2007.

Chapter 4

Ulrich, Dave, and Norm Smallwood. "Capitalizing on Capabilities." *Harvard Business Review* (June 2004): 119–27.

Ulrich, Dave, Wayne Brockbank, Dani Johnson, Kurt Sandholtz, and Jon Younger. *HR Competencies*. Alexandria, VA: Society for Human Resource Management, 2008.

Chapter 5

Boudreau, John, and Peter Ramstad. *Beyond HR: The New Science of Human Capital.* Boston: Harvard Business Press, 2007.

Capelli, Peter. *Talent on Demand: Managing Talent in an Age of Uncertainty.* Boston: Harvard Business Press, 2007.

Cascio, Wayne, and John Boudreau. *Investing in People: Financial Impact of Human Resource Initiatives.* Upper Saddle River, NJ: FT Press, 2008.

Ellig, Bruce. *The Complete Guide to Executive Compensation.* New York: McGraw-Hill, 2001.

Goldsmith, Marshall. "Try Feedforward Instead of Feedback." *Leader to Leader* 25 (Summer 2002): 11–14.

Huselid, Mark, Brian Becker, and Richard Beatty. *The Workforce Scorecard: Managing Human Capital to Execute Strategy.* Boston: Harvard Business Press, 2007.

Lawler, Ed. *Talent: Making People Your Competitive Advantage.* San Francisco: Jossey-Bass, 2008.

Ulrich, Dave, and Wayne Brockbank. *The HR Value Proposition.* Boston: Harvard Business Press, 2005.

Chapter 6

Arvey, Richard, Maria Rotundo, Wendy Johnson, Zhen Zhang, and Matt McGue. "Genetic and Environmental Components of Leadership Role Occupancy." Paper presented at the 21st Annual SIOP (Society of Industrial and Organizational Psychology) conference, Dallas, Texas, April 2006.

Bouchard, Thomas J., Jr., David T. Bouchard, Matthew McGue, Nancy L. Segal, and Auke Tellegen. "Sources of Human Psychological Differences: The Minnesota Study of Twins Reared Apart." *Science*, October 12, 1990.

Harris, Judith Rich. *The Nurture Assumption: Why Children Turn out The Way They Do.* New York: Free Press, 1998.

———. "Where Is the Child's Environment? A Group Socialization Theory of Development." *Psychological Review* 102, no. 3 (July 1995): 458–89.

Lombardo, Michael, and Robert Eichinger. *The Leadership Machine*. Minneapolis: Lominger, 2002.

———. *The Leadership Architect: Norms and Validity Report*. Minneapolis: Lominger, 2003.

Quinn, Ryan, and Wayne Brockbank. "The Development of Human Resource Professionals at BAE Systems." *Human Resource Management* 45, no. 3 (Fall 2006): 477–94.

Ulrich, Dave. *Human Resource Champions*. Boston: Harvard Business Press, 1997.

———. "Coaching for Results." *Business Strategy Series* 9, no. 3 (2008): 104–14.

Ulrich, Dave, Wayne Brockbank, Dani Johnson, and Jon Younger. "Human Resource Competencies: Responding to Increased Expectations." *Employment Relations Today* 34, no. 3 (2007): 1–12.

Chapter 7

Ulrich, Dave, Wayne Brockbank, Dani Johnson, Kurt Sandholtz, and Jon Younger. *HR Competencies*. Alexandria, VA: Society for Human Resource Management, 2008.

Recommended Reading

In addition to the references we cited throughout the text (above), we also recommend the following supplemental reading:

Phase 1

Charan, Ram. *Leadership in the Era of Economic Uncertainty: The New Rules for Getting the Right Things Done in Difficult Times*.

———. *What the CEO Wants You to Know: How Your Company Really Works*.

Christensen, Clayton. *The Innovator's Dilemma*.

Friedman, Thomas. *Hot, Flat, and Crowded*.

———. *The World Is Flat*.

Hamel, Gary and C. K. Prahalad. *Competing for the Future.*

Hamel, Gary. *The Future of Management.*

Heath, Chip. *Made to Stick: Why Some Ideas Survive and Others Die.*

Kim, Chan and Renee Mauborgne. *Blue Ocean Strategy.*

Mintzberg, Henry. *Mintzberg on Management.*

———. *Tracking Strategies.*

Porter, Michael. *Competitive Advantage.*

———. *Competitive Strategy.*

Prahalad, C. K. and Venkat Ramaswamy. *The Future of Competition: Co-Creating Unique Value with Customers.*

Saloner, Garth, Andrea Shepard, and Joel Podolny. *Strategic Management.*

Ulwick, Anthony. *What Customer's Want: Using Outcome-Driven Innovation to Create Breakthrough Products and Services.*

Walker, Gordon. *Competitive Strategy.*

Phase 2

Charan, Ram and Larry Bossidy. *Execution.*

Galbraith, Jay. *Designing Your Organization.*

Hesselbein, Frances, Marshall Goldsmith, and Richard Beckhard. *Organization of the Future.*

Kotter, John. *A Sense of Urgency.*

Lawler, Edward. *Built to Change: How to Achieve Sustained Organization Effectiveness.*

———. *From the Ground Up: Six Principles for Building the New Logic Corporation.*

———. *Talent: Making People Your Competitive Advantage.*

———. *Ultimate Advantage.*

Nadler, David A., Marc S. Gerstein, and Robert B. Shaw. *Organizational Architecture: Designs for Changing Organizations.*

Senge, Peter. *Fifth Discipilne.*

Ulrich, Dave and Dale Lake. *Organization Capability.*

Ulrich, Dave and Norm Smallwood. *Capitalizing on Capabilities.*

Phase 3

Becker, Brian, Mark Huselid, and Dave Ulrich. *HR Scorecard*.

Boudreau, John. *Beyond HR*.

———. *Talent*.

Capelli, Peter. *Talent on Demand*.

Cascio, Wayne. *Investing in People*.

Huselid, Mark, Brian Becker, and Dick Beatty. *The Differentiated Workforce*.

Joyce, William, Nitin Nohria, and Bruce Roberson. *What Really Works: The 4+2 Formula for Sustained Business Success*.

Ulrich, Dave and Wayne Brockbank. *HR Value Proposition*.

Ulrich, Dave. *HR Champions*.

Phase 4

Bridges, William. *Managing Transitions*.

Kerr, Steve. *Reward Systems: Does Yours Measure Up? (Memo to the CEO)*

Kotter, John. *Leading Change*.

INDEX

ABOUT THE AUTHORS

Dave Ulrich

Dave Ulrich is a professor of business at the Ross School of Business, University of Michigan, and cofounder of The RBL Group. He has written 15 books covering topics in HR and leadership, including *HR Champions, HR Value Proposition, HR Competencies, Results Based Leadership: How Leaders Build Value, Leadership Brand*, and *Leadership Code*. He is currently on the Board of Directors for Herman Miller, is a Fellow in the National Academy of Human Resources, and is on the Board of Trustees of Southern Virginia University.

Dave emphasizes defining organizations through the capabilities they possess. His work has helped define and shape key capabilities such as change, learning, collaboration, accountability, talent, service, innovation, and efficiency. The outcomes of leadership and HR are the capabilities that an organization possesses that deliver value to customers, investors, and communities.

Although he has been involved in large-scale research projects, most of his writing is characterized by synthesizing complex ideas into frameworks and tools that executives can use. He is a well-traveled speaker, working with groups of all sizes where he is known for engaging the participants, helping to translate the ideas into actions that work for them. His motto is that good teaching is not what he knows, but how his knowledge helps participants do what they do better.

Dave Ulrich has been ranked the #1 Management Educator and Guru by *BusinessWeek*, selected by *Fast Company* as one of the 10 most innovative and creative leaders, and named the most influential person in HR by *HR Magazine* for three years.

Justin Allen

Justin is the Managing Director of the RBL Institute and a consultant with the RBL Group. He is dedicated to advancing the fields of leadership and strategic HR by connecting leaders with practical tools, leading edge theory, and opportunities to learn from each other.

In the RBL Institute, Justin collaborates with HR leaders from the top companies in the world, including: P&G, Goldman Sachs, Mars, Unilever, Abu Dhabi Investment Authority, LG, Wal-Mart, Nokia, IBM, Royal Bank of Scotland, BNP Paribas, Gap, Rogers, Westpac, and several others. The mission of the RBL Institute is to provide a forum for the world's leading HR strategists to generate ideas, share best practices, and participate in research. Participants have dubbed the RBL Institute as the world's "#1 think tank" for human resources strategy.

Prior to joining the RBL Group, Justin was consistently ranked "top talent" at GE as an HR manager in a diverse business unit where he oversaw performance management, leadership development, staffing, communications, and union relations. Justin also held a variety of other positions at GE, including a training and development role at GE Crotonville and an operations manager role in Ciudad Juarez, Mexico.

Justin began his career as an international researcher in labor statistics and then earned a master's degree in business management and organizational behavior from Brigham Young University. Justin has enjoyed living around the world (Europe, Middle East, and North and South America) and loves going on adventures with his wife, Emily, and their two girls and two boys.

Wayne Brockbank

Wayne Brockbank is a principal of the RBL Group and a Clinical Professor of Business at the University of Michigan's Ross School of Business. At the Ross School of Business, Dr. Brockbank is the Director of the Center for Strategic HR Leadership and the Faculty Director and Core Instructor of the Strategic Human Resource Planning Program, the Human Resource Executive Program, and the Advanced Human Resource Executive Program. He is also the Director of HR executive programs in Hong Kong, Singapore, United Arab Emirates, and India, as well as the Michigan Global Program in Management Development in India.

Professor Brockbank completed his Ph.D. at UCLA and received his Bachelor of Arts and Master of Organizational Behavior from Brigham Young University.

His research and consulting focus on linkages between human resource practices and business strategy, creating high performance corporate cultures, and implementing business strategy through leadership.

Professor Brockbank has consulted in these areas with corporations on every continent, including General Electric, Royal Mail, Cathay Pacific Airways, Unilever, Harley-Davidson, Citigroup, United Bank of Switzerland, Microsoft, IBM, British Telecom, Abu Dhabi Investment Authority, Perez Co., Ericsson, ICI, Godrej Group, Cardinal Health, Deutsche Bank, RGMI, Medtronic, Rolls Royce, Verizon, Australian Public Service Commission, Walt Disney Corporation, General Motors, Saudi Aramco, Texas Instruments, BP, International Paper, Wal-Mart, Goldman Sachs, and Hewlett-Packard.

Dr. Brockbank has participated in dozens of workshops, including workshops with the Academy of Management, Linkage, The Conference Board, SHRM, Singapore Civil Service and others.

Jon Younger

Jon Younger is a principal of the RBL Group, leads the strategic HR practice, and is a director of the RBL Institute. His consulting and executive education work focuses on helping HR departments and HR leaders and professionals play a more strategic role in their organizations. He has worked with a wide range of companies around the world, including AXA, Duke Energy, ING, GE, Takeda Pharmaceuticals, Novartis, Ontario Teacher's Pension Plan (OTPP), United Technologies, Textron, Statoil Hydro, PricewaterhouseCoopers, and Hewitt Associates.

Jon's career has been a mix of consulting, executive management and HR leadership. Prior to joining the RBL Group, he was Chief Learning and Talent Officer of National City Corporation where he was responsible for the leadership development, corporate learning, staffing, performance and talent management, and succession planning. He has also managed executive compensation and HR strategy. He was a cofounder and managing partner of the Novations Group, a strategy implementation and leadership development firm. He also worked briefly as the executive vice president and COO of NetValue U.S. and led a global internal consulting team for Exxon Corporation.

Jon is a coauthor of two books, and has coauthored a variety of articles published in the *Harvard Business Review*, *HR Planning*, *HRM Journal*, and many industry publications. He has taught in the executive education programs of many business schools and corporate universities. His Ph.D. in Organization and Social Psychology is from the University of Toronto. He and his wife, Carolyn, live in Short Hills, N.J.

Mark Nyman

Mark, a principal with the RBL group, has spent his career assisting organizations in transforming themselves by creating strategic focus and then aligning the design of their organizations and systems to carry out this focus. He uses high involvement as a way of building ownership and helps his clients think differently about the issues that challenge them.

Before becoming an external consultant, Mark held several internal consulting positions. He was Director of Business Transformation at Media One where he worked on business restructuring and assisted in the integration and leadership team start-up associated with the AT&T acquisition. He also worked for Amoco where he was the lead consultant in the redesign and transformation of several businesses and acquisitions. Mark was also involved in the redesign of key human resource systems to create better business focus. At Rockwell International, Mark worked in a corporate role supporting large-scale change efforts throughout the company. He also worked in Rockwell's printing press business where he oversaw organization effectiveness and leadership training.

Mark has worked with numerous clients including Adidas, American Century, Cisco, Comcast, Denver Children's Hospital, Honeywell, Johns Manville, Kellogg, Landmark Graphics, Pfizer, Rio Tinto, RR Donnelly, Saudi Aramco, Shell Oil, Sun Microsystems, Occidental Oil and Gas, and Williams Energy. He has a Master's Degree from Brigham Young University in Organizational Behavior where he graduated with high distinction.

ABOUT THE CONTRIBUTORS

Paul Humphries

Mr. Humphries was appointed executive vice president of World Wide Human Resources and Management Systems in 2006, having previously led the global Mechanicals business for six years as SVP Global Operations. In his current role he is responsible for human resources, including worldwide security and corporate responsibility for approximately 80 facilities in 30 countries serving in excess of 200,000 employees. In addition he oversees the development of the company's management systems, which are aimed at creating systemic improvement in the company's core strategic competencies. He previously led their IT and business excellence functions responsible for worldwide deployment of Lean and Six Sigma. In addition he serves as a board member of the Silicon Valley Educational Foundations and is a cochair of the STEM (Science, Technology, Engineerin, and Math) leadership group. He joined Flextronics with the acquisition of Chatham Technologies Inc. in 2000, where he served as senior vice president for global operations responsible for over 30 manufacturing and design facilities across four continents. Prior to joining Flextronics, Mr. Humphries was the managing director for Holts Lloyd Division (EMEA), the Consumer Products Group of Honeywell Corporation, and served as vice president of Operations and Supply Chain for the Autolite Division at Allied Signal/Honeywell. Mr. Humphries previously spent 15 years with Borg Warner Corporation in the UK and US in a variety of HR and business leadership roles. Mr. Humphries was educated in the UK, where he obtained a B.A. in Applied Social Studies and postgraduate qualification in human resource management.

Quinn Wilson

Quinn holds the position of Vice President, Global HR Business Partners (HRBP) at Flextronics. His organization is responsible for driving the strategic HR agenda within Flextronics, including organizational design and effectiveness, senior leadership development, and culture management.

Over the past two years Quinn has participated in leading the Flextronics HR transformation. Specifically, Quinn has worked with the RBL team on developing an HR capability improvement process utilizing the RBL HR competency model. As well, Quinn has worked with his team to develop an HRBP "Toolkit" for use by the global HR team within Flextronics covering topics such as strategic planning, organizational design, workforce planning, communications strategy development, culture management, etc.

Quinn joined Flextronics as part of the Nortel acquisition in 2006 where he had spent nine years in a variety of HR leadership roles supporting their enterprise and wireless global organizations and leading the Canadian HR team. Prior to Nortel, Quinn had worked in the energy sector (BP/Amoco) for over six years. Over the past 18 years, Quinn has held many client facing HR positions as well as HR specialist roles in employee relations, talent acquisition, and compensation and has worked abroad in expatriate roles.

Quinn holds a business degree with a major in human resources and finance from the University of Saskatchewan. Quinn, his wife, Naomi, and their five children live in Calgary, Alberta, Canada.

Chris Altizer

Chris Altizer is Vice President, Human Capital Policy, Pfizer Inc. In this role he is expanding Pfizer's involvement as a major employer in issues of healthcare reform, employment and labor legislation, and related public policy. He is also focused on the improvement of Pfizer's HR function and leads the company's HR redesign project team.

Since joining Pfizer through the acquisition of Warner-Lambert in 2000, Chris has also served in international generalist HR roles spanning Japan, Asia, and Latin America and as Vice President, Global Leadership and Talent Development, which included leading the management development, talent, performance management, and colleague engagement strategies for the enterprise. Prior to joining Pfizer, Chris served in HR generalist and specialist roles at Warner-Lambert and served in various HR and business roles at the Allstate Insurance Company from 1985 to 1997.

Chris holds an M.A.H.R.D. degree from Northeastern Illinois University, an MBA from the Columbia Business School in New York, and a B.A. from Hampden-Sydney College in Virginia. He is a certified scuba diver and a martial arts instructor, a passion he shares with his wife and two sons.

Michele Bolden

Michele Bolden is Vice President, Human Resources, Pfizer Inc. where she is the HR leader responsible for leadership, talent, organizational design, culture, and change for both the worldwide business development and the worldwide HR organizations.

Michele joined Pfizer as human resources director at Ann Arbor laboratories in Ann Arbor, Michigan, as an HR business partner and was promoted to roles of greater responsibility, including as HR leader working with the vice chairman. Prior to joining Pfizer Michele worked in the financial services industry in both general management and HR roles. Michele has a broad and eclectic background, having started her career more than 30 years ago as a public school teacher with subsequent experiences ranging from running a nonprofit to leading the diversity strategy for a major corporation to serving as an ombudsman.

Michele holds a M.H.R.D. from Rutgers University, a M.Ed. from Antioch College in educational administration, and a B.S. in elementary education from Boston University. She has completed the University of Michigan's Advanced Human Resources Program and is a member of SHRM. In her spare time Michele is an active member of the Executive Leadership Council and enjoys travel and the theatre.

Patty Murray

Patricia Murray is senior vice president and director of Intel Corporation's human resources. She is responsible for ensuring the company hires, develops, and retains the best and brightest employees in the industry globally. She is also responsible for providing world class technology-based support and service to Intel's more than 80,000 employees worldwide.

Murray first joined Intel in 1990 as an attorney in the human resources legal staff. She was promoted to manager of the human resources legal staff in 1992, a position she held until her promotion to vice president and director of human resources in 1996. Murray has been a corporate vice president since 1997.

Prior to joining Intel, Murray was an attorney at the law firm of Morrison and Foerster in Palo Alto, California, where she specialized in employment litigation and counseling. Prior to her legal career, Murray was an intensive care unit nurse and nursing administrator at the University of Michigan Hospitals.

Murray was born in Detroit and received a B.A from Michigan State University, a B.S. from Saint Louis University, and a J.D. at the University of Michigan in 1986.

Richard Taylor

Richard Taylor is vice president and director of human resources for Intel Corporation. In this role he oversees all human resources policies and programs for the company worldwide.

Taylor joined Intel in 1986 as European audit manager. From 1989 to 1997 he held positions of United Kingdom finance manager, European controller, controller mobile computing group, and director of operations Europe. In 1998, Taylor was promoted to corporate controller, and in 1999 his duties were extended to include delivery of worldwide employee services.

Prior to joining Intel, Taylor was a corporate auditor for Mobil Oil Corporation from 1981 to 1986. He worked as an audit manager with Deloitte and Touche from 1976 to 1981.

Taylor received his bachelor's degree in psychology from Southampton University in the United Kingdom in 1976. He is a member of the Institute of Chartered Accountants.

Laurene Bentel

Laurene is the Vice President of Human Resources and Administration for Takeda Pharmaceuticals North America, Inc. (TPNA). As a member of the executive team, she is responsible for all aspects of human resources as well as the security and corporate services departments for TPNA and Takeda Global Research & Development Center, Inc. In addition, she consults with and provides guidance to all human resources functions at Takeda San Diego. She is also responsible for supporting and guiding the unique Takeda culture and assuring employee satisfaction.

Prior to being named vice president, Bentel served as senior director of compensation, benefits, and human resource information systems at Takeda, where she led units responsible for the design, implementation, and administration of compensation, benefits, and human resource information systems. Bentel joined Takeda from Grant Thornton, where she served as the director of human resources for the corporate office. While there, Bentel was responsible for coordinating human resource programs, policies, and employee benefit plans.

Previously, Bentel worked at Apollo Travel Services, where she held positions as controller and corporate manager of operating plans. In these roles, Bentel managed capital and expense planning and was also responsible for building, implementing, and improving other planning processes. She also analyzed profitability among Apollo's product lines and built strategic plans for new business ventures.